Dreaming
—the sacred art

Incubating, Navigating & Interpreting Sacred Dreams for Spiritual & Personal Growth

LORI JOAN SWICK, PhD

Walking Together, Finding the Way ®
SKYLIGHT PATHS®
PUBLISHING
Woodstock, Vermont

Dreaming—The Sacred Art:
Incubating, Navigating & Interpreting Sacred Dreams for Spiritual & Personal Growth

2014 Quality Paperback Edition, First Printing

© 2014 by Lori Joan Swick

Library of Congress Cataloging-in-Publication Data available upon request.

10 9 8 7 6 5 4 3 2 1

Manufactured in the United States of America

Cover Design: Jenny Buono
Cover Art: © Shutterstock/Blackspring
Interior Design: Tim Holtz

SkyLight Paths, "Walking Together, Finding the Way" and colophon are trademarks of LongHill Partners, Inc., registered in the U.S. Patent and Trademark Office.

SkyLight Paths Publishing is creating a place where people of different spiritual traditions come together for challenge and inspiration, a place where we can help each other understand the mystery that lies at the heart of our existence.
SkyLight Paths sees both believers and seekers as a community that increasingly transcends traditional boundaries of religion and denomination—people wanting to learn from each other, *walking together, finding the way.*

Walking Together, Finding the Way
Published by SkyLight Paths Publishing
A Division of LongHill Partners, Inc.
Sunset Farm Offices, Route 4, P.O. Box 237
Woodstock, VT 05091
Tel: (802) 457-4000   Fax: (802) 457-4004
www.skylightpaths.com

For those who come to me
in my dreams
—and speak to my soul
with enlightenment and love

CONTENTS

Part Four

Sacred Dream Work as a Means of Personal Fulfillment and Spiritual Growth

INTRODUCTION

Dreams have shaped the spiritual history of humankind. The pervasive power of the sacred dream is well documented throughout the scripture and lore of virtually all the world's religions. According to a popular Hindu myth, all of creation is the divine dream of the god Vishnu, flowering forth from his navel as he floats across the sea of reality in his sleep. Siddhartha Gautama Buddha's journey toward enlightenment was marked with auspicious dreams and, as a result, Buddhists throughout history have valued dreams as spiritual guides. For centuries, monks of the Tibetan Bön tradition have practiced self-mastery of lucid dreaming in order to prepare the soul for life after death, and Taoists sought immortality through dream interpretation. In Mesopotamia kings like Gilgamesh were sent important and powerful dreams from the gods, and the Egyptians viewed dreams as sacred portals through which they could communicate with the dead.

In the Hebrew Bible, Jacob's ladder dream established the importance of the dream as a means of revelation and prophecy (Gen. 28:10–22), and Joseph's ability to decipher the pharaoh's dreams elevated the skill of dream interpretation to a religious art (Gen. 41:1–54). In the Christian Gospels, Joseph was visited in dreams by angels who verified Mary's miraculous virgin pregnancy (Matt. 1:20–24) and who warned him of Herod's plans to destroy the child (Matt. 2:19–22). The significance of Muhammad's night journey dream as the foundation of the

Islamic faith cannot be overstated, nor can the Dreamtime creation story of the Australian Aborigines.

Ideas about what a sacred or mystical dream is vary according to what is culturally or even personally considered sacred. For some people, what is sacred is limited to what is also considered divine, while for others, the sacred can be experienced in the simplest forms of nature, such as the beauty of a perfectly formed leaf, the flight of a bird, the colors of a sunset, or the birth of a child. Within the historical records of sacred dreams from all corners of the world and for this book, sacred dreams are those in which the dreamer experiences the immediate presence or communication from a source he believes is of spiritual or divine origin. For some people, that is understood to be God or Jesus. For others, it could be Allah, the Goddess, or Vishnu, the Tao or "Way," or even pure energy. Because the human experience of the spiritual or sacred is expressed in many different ways, I will refer to it as either the Divine or Ultimate Reality. I am aware these terms still do not capture the essence of spirit (and for that, I offer my sincere apologies), but I find they are acceptable to most people.

In spiritual-presence dreams, the dreamer usually experiences the Divine in the form in which she visualizes it in waking life or as an infusion of pure light. Common divine-communication dreams include visits from deceased love ones, animals, or any variety of metaphorical symbol systems. Sacred dreams are often accompanied by metaphysical experiences, such as feelings of expansiveness, out-of-body travel, and healing. Frequent metacognitive dream gifts include clairvoyance and prophecy.

Dream researcher Kelly Bulkeley conducted a study on spiritual dreaming for the American Psychological Association. He discovered that most people describe their most memorable dream as a mystical one. He underscored the significance of this study by claiming he had found sufficient data to conclude about half of people have mystical dreams.[1] In light of Bulkeley's findings, that Western religious scholars have largely neglected this vast and fascinating arena of human experience is staggering. (Eastern scholars and mystics long ago developed sophisticated systems for exploring dreams as a sacred art.) I suggest the reason for this lies in the fact that the Western academics have worked hard to secularize their religious and scientific research. Once the scientific study of dreaming was relegated to the field of psychology, its spiritual dimensions were left to languish on the laboratory table. The purpose of this book is to help bridge this gap.

My aim is to celebrate the dream experience as a high form of sacred art by providing a useful guide to those who now have spiritual dreams or wish to cultivate the ability to experience them. The techniques I present for incubating, navigating, and working with sacred dreams are based on those I have learned from a variety of spiritual dream traditions and adapted for use in sacred dreaming seminars. I undertake this task as a frequent dreamer of dreams I perceive to be of sacred or spiritual significance and as one with formal training in religion, philosophy, and the spiritual and artistic dimensions of dreaming.

I started experiencing vivid lucid dreams—or dreams in which I was aware of the fact that I was dreaming—after I had surgery as an adolescent. Because I did not understand that the brain autonomously turns off the muscles of the body during deep-dream phases of sleep, my awareness of being conscious and not being able to awaken or move my body resulted in a pattern of frequent night terrors. As I grew older and learned more about the lucid dream state, I eventually trained myself to control the initial instinct to prematurely yank my mind and body from the dream state, and allowed myself to drift through the dream with a sense of adventure. In time I developed a greater sense of reflectiveness—or thoughtful control—in my dream sequences, which often resulted in experiences of expansiveness, communion, and self-transcendence.

In my studies on the psychology and history of religious dreaming, I have discovered my journey of dream awareness is not unique. Sacred dreamers from religious and cultural traditions throughout the world have shared that their experiences often began in youth during an illness or injury that left them bedridden for a period of time. During the deep sleep of recovery, the line between the waking and dream worlds tends to soften and in some instances slips away entirely. In many indigenous cultures the shamans, or medicine men or women, of the community obtain their status by healing themselves from a physical trauma through sacred dreams. Community members perceive that the shamans have been gifted with the ability to receive and decode occult messages from the spiritual dream realm.

Other sacred dreamers have been initiated into the process through other circumstances and report a wide variety of spiritual dreaming experiences, including communion with what they perceive as divine, visitations from the deceased, telepathy, precognition, clairvoyance, prophecy, and out-of-body dream travel. In short, a person who has mastered the art of sacred dreaming is able to transcend the physical barriers of time and space.

In addition, the art of sacred dreaming has tremendous potential as a source of self-healing. In a scientific study, dream-study pioneer Fariba Bogzaran asked lucid dreamers to incubate dreams of their concept of divinity. She found reason to affirm the therapeutic value of lucid dreaming for waking life in that it can lead an individual to reflect on her behavior; work through psychological concerns, problems, dysfunctional patterns, and unfinished business; practice creativity; cultivate more lightness and joy; and evolve toward spiritual awakening.[2]

People of Western consciousness are on the brink of an age when we can expand on our scientific discoveries about human dreaming with a rich variety of cultural and personal sacred experiences. Many of us are awakening to the spiritual depths and wonders of our dreamselves. I write this book in a sincere effort to create space for us to share these dreams, and, by borrowing on the techniques of those who have historically been proficient in sacred dreaming, to provide a practical guide to nurturing sacred dreaming as an art. From my experience guiding myself and others through this process, I have no doubt that those who practice this art can learn to explore their dreams to further their own spiritual potential, and to bring about self-understanding and healing that is often more sophisticated and effective than any therapy available in conversation with another or off the pharmacy shelf.

THE STRUCTURE OF THIS BOOK

This book is designed to facilitate sacred dreaming through four steps: entering sacred dream space, dreaming as a sacred experience, interpreting the dream as a sacred art, and using sacred dream work as a means of spiritual growth and personal fulfillment. In each step, I will explore noteworthy historical and cultural dreamwork methods and rituals and provide a guide for practicing sacred dream techniques.

In part one, I will compare and contrast the activity of human consciousness during waking sacred experiences and sleeping sacred awareness. I will explore ways some dreamers have trained themselves to direct their dreams into the spiritual realm by incubating sacred dream intentions before falling asleep and traversing the hypnogogic state—the mysterious quasi-conscious world one passes through while falling asleep—without losing mindfulness of their intended sacred dream.

The second part of this book will focus on the sacred dreaming experience itself. In this section I analyze occurrences sacred dreamers have reported as well as techniques for discerning the purpose of the prominent sacred dream presence. Because the majority of dreams that dreamers have experienced as sacred or mystical are also lucid dreams, in this section I will share methods of incubating sacred lucid dreams and navigating the dreaming self through such dreams.

Part three focuses on the art of sacred dream interpretation. In this section I share techniques for remembering dreams after waking and ways of recording and working with them to discern their deeper meanings. Because we dream in metaphor, including in sacred dreams, I also share an effective method I have developed of decoding significant dream symbols and patterns of symbols. This method is based on the findings of some of the world's foremost depth psychologists and anthropologists.

The final part of this book delves into the many ways sacred dreamers have turned their sacred dreams into waking life sacred experiences through various forms of artistic expression and methods of personal introspection and self-healing. When working creatively with my own sacred dreams and listening to the testimonies of other sacred dreamers who express their dreams artistically, I have noticed what I call a sacred dream–sacred art feedback loop. The act of reliving the sacred dream while expressing it through art often leads the dreamer into deeper sacred dream sequences that can spiral into new spiritual awareness, healing, and growth. I also discuss some interesting nuances of gender that have been observed in the art of sacred dreaming.

Sacred dream work offers infinite and exhilarating possibilities, and I cannot treat the subject in its entirety in this relatively brief introduction. Therefore, my hope is that this volume will open the way for further discussion and experimentation—especially in Western consciousness. Without a doubt, people of all times and places have had the capacity to dream the sacred, and I assert that to reach our full human potential, we must continue to find creative, self-affirming, and culturally enriching ways to honor and work with these dreams as an eloquent and elevated form of sacred art.

Part One

Entering Sacred
Dream Space

CHAPTER ONE

THE ART OF CULTIVATING SACRED DREAMS

The art of orienting the mind toward dreaming in an intended manner before falling asleep is commonly called dream incubation. Before attempting to incubate our sacred dreams, however, we must understand what the dreaming mind is. Any student of the humanities will know that achieving such understanding is no small undertaking, for the definition of the human mind has been debated by scholars throughout history. Western scientists have largely regarded the mind as the biological brain, while philosophers and theologians have linked the reasoning faculties of the brain with various concepts of the human soul. Aristotle speculated that the mind was housed in the heart, and in the fourth century CE, Augustine of Hippo included the heart as an integral component of the mind in developing his doctrine of the Christian Trinity. Depth psychologists of the twentieth century borrowed the Greek term "psyche"—meaning soul or spirit, as distinguished from body—and developed the notion that the mind is the center of thought, feeling, and behavior, and involves different levels of conscious activity. Spiritual counselor Connie Cockrell Kaplan goes so far as to assert that the womb is the dreaming organ and that the relationship between the womb and the moon controls every aspect of dreaming. This connection creates what she refers to as the Dream Weave that encompasses all human thought and awareness.

So what part or parts of the mind dream? Does dreaming involve the brain, heart, soul, womb, or some integrated combination of these? To prepare the mind for sacred dreaming, we must come to terms with our own ideas about what the dreaming mind is and how it relates to what we hold sacred. From my own experience as a sacred dreamer as well as the testimonies of those who have shared their sacred dream experiences with me, I believe spiritual dreaming can involve every level of brain activity and consciousness.

For me, dreaming is also an embodied phenomenon. Although a distinction must be made between the sensations of the physical waking life body and those of the dream body, I am certain the sacred dream can involve either and often greatly affects both. However, I believe the human soul drives sacred dreaming. I understand the soul to be a divinely bestowed facility for participation in the sacred web that pervades all existence. From this perspective, I have developed my own methods of sacred dream incubation as cultivation of consciousness, body, and soul to enter the sacred dream realm. My approach reflects the sacred dream incubation practices that have been documented throughout history.

HISTORICAL METHODS OF SACRED DREAM INCUBATION

The oldest written references to dream incubation were recorded on cuneiform tablets by the Mesopotamians as far back as 3000 BCE. In "The Interpretation of Dreams in the Ancient

Near East, With a Translation of an Assyrian Dream-Book,"
A. Leo Oppenheim, professor of Assyriology at the University
of Chicago's Oriental Institute, explains that Sumerian, Hittite,
Akkadian, and Assyrian kings incubated dreams to access and
interpret messages from deities. One ruler who sought a message dream offered this prayer as part of his incubation ritual:

> Reveal thyself to me and let me behold a favorable dream.
> May the dream that I dream be favorable; may the dream
> that I dream be true. May Makhir, the goddess of dreams,
> stand at my head, let me enter the temple of the gods and
> the house of life.[1]

After reciting the invocation, the ruler would enter a temple
or sanctuary dedicated to the dream deity, perform a variety of
preparatory rituals, and sleep in the temple all night.

A classic example of this practice was recorded in *The Epic
of Gilgamesh*. As the King of Sumeria, Gilgamesh sought divine
guidance through sacred dream incubation in his attempts to
evade death. Though the texts are fragmented, the pith of his
request can be discerned: "I lift my head to pray to the moon
god Sin: For ... a dream I go to the gods in prayer ... preserve
me!"[2] Unfortunately, the gods did not honor Gilgamesh's
dream request. He lost his kingship and was forced to accept
the condition of human mortality.

A thousand years later, accounts recorded in the Hebrew
Bible show that the ability to incubate auspicious sacred dreams
was still associated with the king's ability to rule. According to
the biblical texts, King Solomon offered a sacrifice and burned
incense at a high place at Gibeon. He spent the night in a shrine
there, during which the Lord appeared to him, granted his
request for understanding and a wise heart, and added riches
and glory beyond that of his royal peers (1 Kings 3:5–14).

Sacred dream incubation was widely practiced in ancient Egypt. Several temples were devoted to the god Serapis, who under the auspices of the goddess Isis was the deity of dreams. One of the main dream temples of Serapis was built at Memphis about 3000 BCE. Some of the incubation rituals included prayers and drawings of the desired dreams. Incantations and dream requests were sometimes placed in the mouth of a mummy or a dead cat, which were believed to be spiritual messengers between the waking and the sacred dream worlds.[3] One sacred dream incubation ritual consisted of the dreamer writing the names of five different deities on a clean linen bag before folding it up, saturating it with oil, and setting it on fire. Before the dreamer went to sleep, he would repeat an incantation seven times and put out the flame.[4]

The Hindu Vedic scriptures devoted much attention to the spiritual aspects of sleep and dreams. The Chandogya Upanishad, which focuses on the search for Ultimate Reality, gives a detailed account of a ritual dream incubation. It instructs a "man who is seeking greatness" to mix certain herbs, honey, and curd on the night of the full moon. He is also advised to pour offerings of clarified butter into fire while praising the gods. Finally, he is to drink the mixture before lying down in front of the flame, where he is advised to remain "silent and unresisting." If he sees a woman in his dreams, she is a sign that his dream incubation has been successful, and he may then ask for the divine fulfillment of a wish.[5]

The ancient Chinese Taoists regularly practiced dream incubation in temples. Their preparatory rituals included burning incense before the temple god. Several accounts attest to judges and other officials incubating dreams in temples for guidance in civil affairs.[6] In the late Ming and Qing dynasties, dream incubation flourished not only in temples, but in graveyards, caves, and wilderness sanctuaries.[7]

In ancient Greece and Rome, the art of dream incubation reached its pinnacle as a cultural phenomenon at the temples of the dream god, Asclepius. For centuries, dreamers seeking healing, prophecy, and wisdom made pilgrimages to sleep in one of these temples. Most of them were set in beautiful, remote settings with a large statue of Asclepius standing at the entrance. Nonpoisonous snakes, familiars of the god, wandered the grounds freely. The incubation procedures for a healing sacred dream were elaborate and varied from temple to temple. Standard rituals demanded that the dreamer follow a special diet, refrain from sexual intercourse, take frequent walks in fresh air, and bathe often in cold water. In some temples, animals (usually rams) were ritually sacrificed, and dreamers would sleep on the animals' skins. Before dreamers retired for the night, a formal sacred rite known as the "hour of the sacred lamps" was officiated by Asclepian priests, including hymns and prayers in which the god was asked to grant sacred dreams. Finally, the temple priests would escort the dreamers into an inner sanctum of the temple and instruct them to lie down on a *kline*, a ritual bed. Snakes slithered on the floor around them while they slept. According to the many testimonials recorded on the temple walls, the typical sacred dream consisted of a visit from Asclepius or one of his daughters, Hygeia or Panacea, who gave firsthand instruction on what kind of medicine or curative treatment should be administered. The incubation process could continue for many nights before the dreamer attained the desired results.

The Christian Scriptures and other early Christian texts attest to the notion that sacred dreams could effect favorable spiritual transformations. However, among the many powerful accounts of spiritually charged Christian dreams, few describe sacred dream incubation. The Roman martyrdom account of Saints Perpetua and Felicity shows that Perpetua was considered adept at sacred dream cultivation. During her imprisonment, her brother reminded her that she was divinely favored with the ability to ask for revelations in her dreams and urged her to incubate a dream prophesying the outcome of her trial. She promised she would tell him the results of her sacred dream the next day, confirming that she "knew that she could speak with the Lord."[8] The details of her dream incubation process were not recorded, but because she was confined in a heavily guarded cell with her infant son, we can assume she had little control over the elements of her ritual. She did experience a powerful sacred dream that evening, however, and had subsequent prophetic dreams right up to the day of her execution by wild animals in a Roman amphitheater.

Several accounts of successful dream incubation in Christian churches and cathedrals dedicated to the Virgin Mary have been recorded since the Middle Ages. Interestingly, most commonly the churches are those that house a Black Madonna icon. Saint Ignatius of Loyola had his dramatic Christian conversion experience while sleeping in a pew adjacent to the statue of Our Lady of Montserrat in Barcelona, Spain, and sacred dream incubation is still ardently practiced before the statue of the Black Madonna of Chartres in northern France.

Istikhara is a popular form of Muslim sacred dream incubation. It is still widely practiced, particularly by the Sufis, a mystical sect of Islam. Though it is not mentioned in the Qur'an, it is referred to in several of the minor hadiths, and many Muslims believe it was taught by Muhammad himself. The goal of Istikhara is to seek divine guidance about whether to perform an action in waking life. (A common question is whether a marriage should take place.) Some Istikhara dreamers sleep in mosques, while others perform the rite at the tomb of a religious saint. It can be performed during the day, but is generally believed to be more effective when practiced after the first half of the night has passed. The incubation rite is largely made up of a succession of fervent prayers, beginning with the repentance of sins committed since puberty and a promise to sin no more. Then the dreamer declares her intention to perform Istikhara, sends blessings to the Prophet, makes her intention for the task in question, and lies down on her right side. The dreamer blocks out the world by repeating the name of Allah until she falls asleep.

In his essay "Istikhara and Dreams," professor of Islamic studies Hidayet Aydar explains:

> If these instructions are followed and one envisages the color white or green, a religious leader, peace or tranquility, or pleasant things, then the task will be beneficial; if one envisages black, blue, yellow, or red, unpleasant types of people or repulsive or ugly things, then the outcome is evil.[9]

Sacred dream incubation has been practiced throughout the history of humanity, and the customs I have noted here represent only a fraction of the sacred dream incubation rituals that have been preserved in writing. As disparate as the rituals are in some respects, they do still exhibit many common characteristics that can be examined to gain a deeper appreciation for the nuances of sacred dream incubation practiced to experience Ultimate Reality. Furthermore, I find that an appreciation for these historical rituals can lay the groundwork for the development of contemporary dream incubation methods as a form of sacred art.

THE RITUAL ELEMENTS OF SACRED DREAM INCUBATION

In evaluating the rituals of historical sacred dream interpretation, we see that the predominant prerequisite is the appropriate sacred space. People have commonly sought to perform their sacred dream sleep in the liminal realm between the physical and spiritual realms. Temples and places of natural beauty have been the most obvious choices, because they have already been designated and perhaps consecrated as sacred space. That sacred dream seekers would choose to sleep on or near gravesites may seem macabre, but the relics of those who were considered saints have historically been understood to serve as a bridge between heaven and earth. Caves have traditionally signified the womb of the Earth Mother, and sleeping inside her simulates a spiritual rebirth. From this perspective, incubating a dream within a cave has the potential to produce a host of sacred new beginnings and revelations. I agree with Bulkeley's observation that

> dream incubation requires more than just an emotional concern; it also requires a change in the person's physical sleeping conditions, a reorientation of the body and soul within the broader meaning structures of the cosmos.[10]

For all practical purposes, most contemporary dreamers cannot regularly sleep in temples, cemeteries, or caves. We can, however, create sacred space where we usually sleep and plan to incubate sacred dreams. We should consider Bulkeley's recommendations on sacred dream incubation space:

> Whether practiced in a cave, a temple, a mountain, or desert, or a graveyard, the underlying logic of dream incubation always involves a dramatic shift *away* from one's normal sleep patterns and *toward* an unusual place where the powers of whatever the individual holds as sacred are gathered in especially concentrated form.[11]

For me, few things in life are more exhilarating than creating sacred space, and designing sacred dream space could be the first tangible artistic expression of dream incubation. If you can sleep in another room, you might try arranging a separate dream sanctuary. If not, simply moving the bed could create a dramatic shift from your normal sleep and dream patterns.

The ancient Taoist art of *bagua* holds that the direction your bed faces can have vast effects on the flow of your energy. I recently moved my bed from the back wall of my bedroom, which was across from the double-door entrance to the room. After moving it just a couple of feet, so it faces due north, I was amazed at how differently I felt lying in bed. It removed me from the massive flow of energy that before had seemingly rushed up the stairwell, through the bedroom doorway, across my room, and into my dreams. When the moon is full, the energy streams in through the window to my right during the first half of the night, when my dreams are milder. When the moon is in its first quarter, it peeks in at me from the window on my left during the early hours of the morning, when my dreaming is consistently more intense. Not only do I sleep more soundly, but my dreams are more peaceful as well.

In creating sacred dream space, we should surround it with, as Bulkeley says, whatever you hold as charged with sacred powers. Because I was raised in the Catholic tradition, I have always had an affinity for the Virgin Mother; therefore, I have created an altar with a large painting of Our Lady of Czestochowa, a Black Madonna associated with Poland for nearly six hundred years. She is surrounded with candles, fresh flowers, holy cards, and various Marian gifts I have been presented with throughout the years. On the other side of my sacred dream space, I have a shrine to Guan Yin that miraculously established itself when my son brought me three statues of her from China. I placed a vase with a hydrangea on a table next to my Guan Yins. After two years the flower is still alive and as beautiful as it was the day I bought it, though I stopped watering it well over a year ago. I read somewhere that amethyst crystals are conducive to sacred dreaming, so I keep one on my nightstand. I find I regularly have to move it closer to or farther away from my bed, depending on the position of the moon and the intensity of my dreams.

As part of the sacred dream incubation process, you need to thoughtfully and aesthetically create your own sleep and dream space so that when you relax there, you feel you can easily navigate your mind into the liminal realm between wakefulness and dream, and ultimately from mere physical reality into sacred reality. Like all other worthwhile pursuits, sacred dreaming should be regarded as a process and not a one-time event. Therefore, you should keep your physical dream space fluid—moving, adding, and taking away elements, depending on what seems to enhance or detract from your sacred dreaming experiences. If you feel you are in sacred space while you incubate a dream, you are also much more likely to feel you are in the presence of the sacred within your dream.

Another dream incubation ritual that has been practiced throughout history is purification. Aside from the traditional belief that only what is pure can be in communion with the Divine, practical reasons exist for performing physical cleansing rituals when trying to cultivate sacred dreaming. Scientific study has proven that ingesting heavy meats, sugary foods, alcohol, and some medications before going to bed can greatly disrupt the natural sleep cycle, which can bedevil dream activity. Ritual bathing not only cleans the body, but eases muscle tension. Adding cleansing or relaxing floral or herbal scents or extracts to ritual bathing waters can also help to relieve mental and emotional stress and clear the dreaming mind before the incubation process. Predreaming rituals of repentance and meditation also help clear the mind and soul and make you more susceptible to sacred communication.

Strikingly, almost every historical dream incubation process includes a ritual form of fire. From a mythological perspective, fire symbolizes all the ambivalence associated with divine energy. It warms yet burns. It lights yet consumes. Close observation of a flame can be mesmerizing, and ancient dream incubators could watch their fire sacrifices rise heavenward in smoke. I believe fire is also closely associated with sacred dreaming because what the dreamer perceives to be divine appears in dreams in the form of pure light with amazing regularity. More often than not, dreamers describe this phenomenon as a glowing light more brilliant than fire. For this reason, lighting a candle or incense as part of a dream incubation ritual can be a powerful experience. (Of course, I make sure I do not retire before I extinguish my presleep flame to avoid leaving an unattended flame burning.)

Another common dream incubation ritual is to approach the Divinity with a definite dream request. The manner in which this is offered fluctuates from one incubation ritual to another. In some cases it is merely spoken, while in others it is chanted or sung. Usually the sacred dream intention or question is written down. These are important steps that modern dream incubators tend to ignore. Because normal thinking activity tends to shift rapidly from one concept to another, by merely thinking an intention, the dreamer is apt to inadvertently leave it in an amorphous form. But chanting, reciting, or singing forces us to articulate the intention. Because we usually vocalize our thoughts only to communicate them with someone else, orally offering an intention embodies the dreamer's effort to communicate with the Sacred on a profound level.

The act of writing the sacred dream intention or question, or the name of the deity invoked makes the incubation process even more real and powerful. Writing requires more thought than speaking or singing, and for those of us who were raised in cultures framed by religions based on scripture, the association of the written word with the spiritual cannot be overestimated. After all other dream incubation rituals have been completed, the hopeful dreamer repeats the intention or the name of the deity in the form of a mantra until she drifts off to sleep.

The sacred dream incubation process I have found conducive to sacred dreaming is based on these basic rituals coupled with contemporary scientific methods of dream incubation I have adapted. There are many more historical dream incubation practices, but these are the most common and therefore the most useful in constructing a method for contemporary sacred dream induction.

"Setting the Intention" Dream Incubation

1. Create your dream temple.

Creating a dream temple can be as monumental a project as renovating your sleeping space or as simple as moving one or two objects that are sacred to you closer to your bed. The objective here is that you feel as though you are in a new and sacred place when you lie down to cultivate your sacred dream.

2. Perform sacred dream incubation purification rituals.

Avoid heavy foods, alcohol, and mind-altering drugs during the evening before you cultivate your sacred dream. Make sure the place you plan to sleep is clean. Washing the sheets and whatever you plan to wear to bed contributes to the ritual. White or light-colored bedclothes and sleepwear can also help promote a feeling of purity.

Above all, take a highly ritualized predream bath. A shower is fine but not the same. Relaxing in warm water simulates the feeling of being in the cosmic womb in anticipation of a sacred, new-life experience in much the same way entering a cave assisted ancient sacred dreamers in their incubation rituals. Adding orange peel or ginger to the water can draw toxins out of the body, while lavender and chamomile help induce peaceful sleep. Use whatever combination of herbs, perfumes, or commercial bath salts or scents you associate with the Sacred. But do something different from your usual self-cleaning ritual, and as you soak, be attentive to the fact that you are cleansing not only your body, but your mind and soul as well.

3. Set and declare your dream intention.

After your purification ritual, light a candle. If you like, play music that is soothing and sacred for you. While you watch the flame, set your sacred dream intention. This can be in the form of a problem for which you would like divine guidance, a question for which you would like a divine answer, or simply a request for a dream of divine presence, wisdom, or understanding. Be sure to frame your intention or request in a way that is not too restrictive. If you are open-minded about your encounter with the sacred presence at work in your dreams, you are more likely to experience gifts you never expected. I find this intention a good one to begin with:

Tonight in my dreams I would like to be in the presence of the Divine.

If you would like to personally invoke a specific form of the Divine, that is fine, too. You might even call the Divine by name in your intention, but be sure to word your intention so you are clear that you are open for communication and not demanding or necessarily even expecting it. The tone with which you frame your intention is crucial.

Once your intention is set, recite, chant, or sing it. Feel free to dance or move in any way that reaffirms and honors the sacred nature of your request. Write it down. Be concrete and specific.

You may offer up the written intention by burning it in the flame of your candle, but most sacred dreamers prefer to place the paper under their pillows. Extinguish your candle and lie down.

4. Incubate your sacred dream.

Lie in a comfortable position—preferably on your back, because you can more easily extend your spine, which is important for meditative breathing. Take a deep, comfortable breath and feel it filling your whole body with soft, bright light. Hold the breath momentarily before exhaling slowly. Continue breathing in this manner as you mentally recite your sacred dream intention. If you feel the urge to roll over, do so, but continue to focus on your breathing and the rhythmic recitation of your dream intention until you fall asleep.

Do not be concerned if you cannot immediately incubate a sacred dream. If you wake up in the middle of the night, repeat the breathing and intention-recitation cycle. Dream scientists have affirmed that most people experience longer and deeper rapid eye movement (REM) sleep in the early hours of the morning, and this is also when dreams are the most vivid. Do not be too concerned if you do not experience a sacred dream the first night you try. Just as the Greek and Roman dreamers in the temples of Asclepius sometimes had to pursue their dream intentions for several nights, you might need some time before you achieve the desired results. You might well receive the sacred dream affirmation you sought but not remember it upon waking. Be sure to record any dream scenarios you might recall, even if they do not seem remotely related to your dream intention. Sometimes they turn out to be laden with meaningful symbolism that becomes apparent only with later examination. Techniques for this analysis are described in detail in chapter 6, but whatever you do, do not give up. Through continued practice and perseverance, you will soon be adept at the art of cultivating sacred dreams.

CHAPTER TWO

THE THIN VEIL BETWEEN WAKING AND SLEEPING CONSCIOUSNESS

Over 2,000 years ago, the Taoist sage Chuang Tzu recorded a dream in which he was a butterfly, happily fluttering about. He then pondered whether he was in reality a man dreaming he was a butterfly or a butterfly dreaming he was a man.[1] He articulated a question that has fascinated dreamers throughout the history of humankind. Though most of us see a general correlation between our experiences while awake and in dreams, what is the true connection between the two? While psychologists and sleep scientists struggle to formulate explanations, religious shamans and mystics have developed their own theories and practices, integrating their dreaming and waking life visions and experiences into an organic process of discovering spiritual depth and meaning.

Barbara Tedlock, an initiated Mayan shaman and anthropologist, maintains that dreaming is a universal experience that can occur while you are awake or asleep. She writes that the waking path consists of guided fantasies known as omens, waking dreams, and visions. On the sleeping side are personal dreams (based on everyday events or wishes of the soul), prophetic dreams, archetypal dreams, nightmares, and lucid dreams.[2]

Tedlock says that for people of shamanic traditions, both dreams and visions are valuable sources of prophecy and self-understanding.[3]

The Australian Aboriginal concept of the dreamtime perfectly illustrates the pervasive power of the sacred dream in relation to waking life. In the dreamtime, ancestral spirits created the world, its inhabitants, and landmarks, and left evidence of their sacred intentions. Based on the Western understanding of time, we might think the dreamtime happened only at the beginning of creation, but historian Terry D. Bilhartz explains that to Aborigines, the dreamtime is considered a "timeless eternity that mixes together the past, present, and future" and can be accessed at any moment through communion with the spirit world by way of dreams and sacred rituals.[4] In essence, all of created reality is experienced as part of a timeless sacred dream. Therefore, in this cultural context, in order to understand the natural-spiritual aspects of the self and the world, the spiritual dream is at least as important, if not more important, than waking life ritual.

Tenzin Wangyal Rinpoche, a lama of the Tibetan Bön tradition, says the first step in dream practice is quite simple: "One must recognize the great potential that dream holds for the spiritual journey." In his book *The Tibetan Yogas of Dream and Sleep*, he claims that "there is nothing more real than dream." This makes sense, he says, because of the Tibetan philosophical view that "normal waking life is as unreal as dream, and in exactly the same way."[5]

Buddhist scholar Serinity Young emphasizes the importance of tending to our dreams as a means of positively transforming waking life in general. She claims that "dreams can reveal to an individual insights so powerful that the concerns or realities of waking life are lost in the blinding light of this new awareness." Young adds that such dreams shape a person's reality and her understanding of the waking world.[6]

The Hebrew Bible treats waking visions and dreams as equally important methods of human communication with the Divine. The end of times is foretold in the verse, "And it shall come to pass afterward, that I will pour out my Spirit on all flesh; your sons and your daughters shall prophesy, your old men shall dream dreams, and your young men shall see visions" (Joel 2:28). This apocalyptic warning is repeated in the Christian Scriptures in the Book of Acts (2:17). Why sons and daughters will prophesy, old men will dream dreams, and young men will see visions, in that particular order, is a matter of exegetical debate. Significantly, however, the sacred messages that are to be dispensed will be deemed just as real and important in the sleeping dream as in the waking vision. The Hebrew prophet Daniel "had understanding in all visions and dreams" (Dan. 1:17); and the Hebrew and Christian Scriptures honor both as means of sacred communication and do not seem to value one more highly than the other.

Though psychologists, shamans, and mystics may never come to a consensus about where or how wide the line between waking and sleeping consciousness is, I have formulated at least working answers to two questions I believe are crucial in developing a fruitful practice of dreaming as a sacred art. First, what is the relationship between waking sacred thoughts, visions, or experiences, and sleeping sacred dreams? Second, how can a person develop continuity between the two in order to enhance his personal and spiritual life?

WAKING AND DREAM CONSCIOUSNESS

Many studies have been conducted and theories formulated about how and why the brain produces dreams in sleep. Though a comprehensive review of this work is outside the scope of this book, to understand how sacred dream consciousness relates to waking spiritual consciousness, we should note that all people have a sleep cycle, which for most teenagers and adults repeats every 90 to 100 minutes. Therefore, during a night of sleeping six to eight hours, most people go through four or five sleep cycles.

J. Allan Hobson, professor of psychiatry at Harvard Medical School and director of the Laboratory of Neuropsychology at Massachusetts Mental Health Center, reports that within each sleep cycle are four possible types of sleep. He writes:

> Stage 1 is a light sleep, Stage 2 deeper, Stage 3 deeper still, and Stage 4 the deepest. Each cycle usually begins with a quick descent through Stage 1 into Stage 2, then 3 or 4, and ends after an ascent back up, followed by a stretch of Stage 1 sleep.[7]

Hobson goes on to explain that in the deepest sleep of Stage 4, brain activity is limited; heart rate, respiration, and body temperature are at their lowest; and we do not dream. Stages 3 and 2 are similar but less extreme. In Stage 1 sleep, when the brain becomes very active and the heart and respiration rates increase significantly, we are most likely to dream.[8] In this stage, the brain releases chemicals that restrict muscular activity throughout the body (as a natural means of self-protection from acting out our dreams), except for the eyes, which watch the images that pass through the dream. For this reason, sleep and dream researchers refer to the first phase of sleep as REM (rapid eye movement) sleep. Electroencephalography (EEG) can record the electrical wave patterns of eye movements and brain activity during sleep.

Particularly interesting are the findings of EEG studies that during the REM stage of sleep, when dreams are most likely to occur, the EEG patterns of eye movement are similar to those of a person who is awake. Psychologist Susan Blackmore reports that

in REM sleep the brain is highly active and the EEG resembles that of waking, although, paradoxically, the sleeper is harder to waken than during non-REM sleep. Even in non-REM sleep the overall firing rate of neurons is as high as in waking states, but the pattern is quite different, with EEG dominated by long slow waves rather than complex fast ones.[9]

These findings indicate that while dreaming during the first or REM stage of sleep, the brain's activity is amazingly similar to its activity in waking life. In fact, it is so intense that it is more difficult for the dreamer to transition from the dream state to the waking state in the first phase than in other phases of sleep. We should note that while dream researchers find that the first stage of sleep is the most conducive to active dreaming, EEG studies show that dreaming does occur in the second and third stages of non-REM sleep, when brain activity can be high but not the same as in waking states.

From this research, we can see that according to the normal sleep cycle, when we fall asleep we usually enter REM sleep first; move through stages 2, 3, and 4; and then end the cycle with a longer phase of REM. Therefore, any continuity of consciousness from waking to dreaming states would appear to be most easily cultivated between the waking consciousness as it transitions through the hypnogogic state and enters the initial REM stage of the sleep cycle and from the final REM stage of the sleep cycle as it transitions back into waking consciousness. However, since the brain has the most difficulty transitioning from REM sleep to the waking state, what we need is a sacred portal between the two.

Perhaps remarkably, 3,500 years before Western psychologists and scientists developed their theories on sleep and dream stages, Hindu Scripture described four states of consciousness. The Mandukya Upanishad names the first state of consciousness *Vaishvanara,* in which "one lives with all the senses turned outward, aware only of the external world." The second state is called *Taijasa.* It is "the dreaming state in which, with the senses turned inward, one enacts the impressions of past deeds and present desires." Those who master this stage of their dreams, this Upanishad maintains, "become established in wisdom. In their family everyone leads the spiritual life." The third state, *Prajna,* is the state of deep sleep "in which one neither dreams nor desires. There is no mind in *Prajna*, there is no separateness; but the sleeper is not conscious of this." The author of this text adds, "Let him become conscious in *Prajna* and it will open the door to the state of abiding joy." The fourth state is *Turiya,* which is "neither inward nor outward, beyond the senses and the intellect." It is in this state that you become one with the Divine and know infinite peace and love.[10]

Though the states of the waking-sleeping consciousness described in this Upanishad do not perfectly match those proposed by contemporary psychologists and scientists, there are some amazing parallels. The Mandukya Upanishad follows a pattern of consciousness from the waking state to a dream state that is similar to REM dream sleep and perhaps encompasses the second and third stages of sleep as well. It also recognizes a deeper, dreamless sleeping state. The fourth state seems to transcend waking or dreaming consciousness. In this phase we experience the ultimate state of self-actualization and joy.

Of particular interest here is that the Hindu philosophy concerning states of waking and dream consciousness is based not on scientific research, but on a purely spiritual awareness. And the sacred portal that leads through all four states is the mantra symbol *aum*, which stands for Supreme Reality. In essence, this Upanishad is a meditative practice that instructs us to clear the waking mind of everything but the aum of Supreme Reality. In traditional yogic practice the Hindu symbol for aum is usually visualized, while the "syllables" A-U-M are chanted in tandem with a rhythmic pattern of meditative breathing. The goal is to train the consciousness to stay attentive to aum while it passes through the stages of dream and nondream sleep until union with the Divine is reached.

But is such a thing humanly possible? Dream psychologist Tracey L. Kahan writes that though Western sleep scientists have assumed the dreaming mind was incapable of metacognitive skills such as self-reflection, intentionality, and self-regulation, several recent sleep and dream studies have proven that during REM-stage dreaming, and especially during lucid dreaming, such skills are possible and

> can be increased simply by increasing one's attention to the reporting of dreams and reinforcing the intention to notice the process or content characteristics of one's dreams.[11]

Kahan also states that dream studies support the belief that a feedback loop between waking and dreaming states, mediated by attention and intention, can coevolve.[12] In other words, as the Mandukya Upanishad proclaimed, those who practice the art of intending to dream about a specific thing or concept before going to sleep and reflecting on that same thing or concept after waking can train themselves to follow a stream of cognitive clarity throughout the natural cycle of waking and dreaming states of consciousness. What is significant about forming a conscious continuum between sacred waking visions and sacred dreams from the standpoint of the Upanishads, as well as from modern scientific research, is that the sacred portal between the two exists and can be accessed with sacred dream practice and conviction.

Although some of us who were raised with a Western view of consciousness might have difficulty believing it is possible to develop the ability to maintain cognitive control through all states of waking and sleeping consciousness in the manner described in the Mandukya Upanishad, religious history attests that is has been accomplished. Confucian texts tell of the seventeenth-century Qing scholar Wei Xiang-shu, who wrote that he could "hold his own" while dreaming. As he describes the process, he seems to have been able to order his mind's activity throughout the waking and sleeping states of consciousness.[13]

With this in mind, how are we to articulate the relationship between waking sacred thoughts, visions, or experiences, and sleeping sacred dreams so that this expression can serve as a practical guide for those who want to experience dreaming as form of sacred art today? Based on historical testimony as well as my own experience with sacred dreaming and that of those who have shared with me in seminars, retreats, and workshops, I believe the experience of the sacred vision, voice, or sensation in waking life can be of the same psychological and spiritual essence as the sacred dream of sleep. The key to making the connection between the two lies in the attitude and determination of the individual. Someone who is open to connecting her waking sacred experiences with her sacred dream experiences is much more likely to enjoy the fruits of both as an integral aspect of her spiritual life. And, I am convinced, anyone who takes the time and makes the effort to cultivate, navigate, and interpret her sacred dreams can and will find the portal between the two and travel through it often. I like Connie

Cockrell Kaplan's definition of dreaming as "a direct encounter with energy in the dimension of truth." This concept of the nature of the dream leaves her room to assert that *dreaming may occur in both waking and sleeping consciousness."*[14]

Professor of consciousness studies Allan Combs's concept of human consciousness also sheds light on how waking experiences relate to dream experiences. In his book *The Radiance of Being*, he reminds us that consciousness, as the essence of human experience, is always *about* something. He writes, "Thus consciousness is always in the business of bringing objects into awareness, whether through thoughts, dreams, memories, feelings, or sensory impressions such as tastes, sounds, and visual images. In other words, consciousness always has a point." In formal terms, Combs says, consciousness is intentional, and "like a polarizing magnetic field that draws iron fillings into formations of multiple ellipses, consciousness aligns the processes of the mind into patterns with direction and purpose."[15] Combs's description of the work of the consciousness does much more than just explain why we often dream about what has been preoccupying our minds before we go to sleep. It also helps to answer the age-old question that has been recently well articulated by the popular recording artist Seal, "Why must we dream in metaphor?"

If the mind works on its intentions by pulling them into patterns of meaning, we should not be surprised that although our dreams sometimes seem to be conveying an explicit storyline, they are virtually always layered with patterns of symbols. These symbols carry deeper meanings and associations that are aimed at helping our conscious or unconscious work out answers to the intentions it is focused on. Therefore, if someone has sacred intentions in waking life, he will have spiritual dreams while sleeping. The sacred portal between the two lies in understanding the patterns or systems of symbols of your most sacred conscious intentions.

DEVELOPING CONTINUITY BETWEEN WAKING SACRED EXPERIENCE AND SLEEPING SACRED DREAMS

Depth psychologist Carl Jung was fascinated with the power of symbols in dreams and how they could be used to align the unconscious aspect of dreams with the conscious brain activity of waking life in order to achieve what he called individuation—a balanced psychic self. Jung pointed out that a psychological connection exists between the symbolic content of dreams and the symbolic content of mythology, or stories upon which the world's religions are based. I think this parallel is crucial for relating waking spiritual awareness to the symbols of sacred dreams.

In his study "Symbols and the Interpretations of Dreams," Jung wrote, "Dream symbols are for the most part manifestations of a psyche that is beyond the control of consciousness."[16] In the same way, symbols in religious stories also represent deeper meanings or cultural values of the community that adhere to the truth of the story. For example, many creation myths contain a serpent. Serpents are also common motifs in dreams people consider sacred. Sigmund Freud taught that common mythological and dream symbols are "archaic remnants" or vestiges of human remembrance that are imprinted on our consciousness as a human inheritance from one generation to another. Jung borrowed from Freud's theory and taught that we all draw on a human fund of what he called "primordial images" or "archetypes" that recur with amazing similarity in the mythology and dreams of individuals throughout time and history.

While I do not know if I completely agree with Freud and Jung that dream archetypes or symbols are psychic imprints of our ancestors, I do believe the connection between them, and between one human mind and another, awake and dreaming, is real. For example, anyone who grew up in a place with a pervasive Jewish or Christian culture, even if he himself was not

Jewish or Christian, would be familiar with the role of the serpent in the story of Adam and Eve in the Garden of Eden. He also probably would have seen versions of this story depicted in art in many different ways and on different occasions. Because in this particular story, the serpent is deceitful, manipulative, and harmful, we would expect that if this person dreamed of an encounter with a serpent, he would experience it as deceitful, manipulative, and harmful. Many people who relate dreams about serpents they perceive as sacred, however, despite having been raised in cultures predominately influenced by biblical stories, sense that the snake in their dreams is a symbol of growth, healing, and new beginnings. Why?

According to depth psychologists, the answer relates to the fact that in ancient civilizations the serpent was also a pervasive symbol of healing and regeneration. Even today, the symbol for healing professions in the modern Western world is the caduceus—two serpents entwined on a winged pole that was a symbol associated with the Roman god, Hermes. Hermes was the god of cunning and theft, and conductor of the dead into Hades, much like the satanic serpent in the Garden of Eden. However, he was also the god of commerce and invention, and the patron of travelers and rogues. As I mentioned, snakes wandered freely in the healing dream temples of Asclepius in Greece. But even before serpents became symbols of the Roman and Greek gods, they were associated with the great goddesses of birth, death, and the continual regeneration of nature. No doubt this connection has to do with the fact that a snake in its natural habitat can both slide below the ground (as if it is going to Hades) and slither up a tree, connecting heaven and earth. In addition, it can slough its skin, looking as though it is rebirthing itself. Whether common sacred dream symbols like serpents or the aum of reality are carried in our unconsciousness as archaic remnants, as Freud and Jung contended, or they have somehow subliminally sneaked into our psyches from a barrage of subtle cultural messages, they function in dreams.

Of course, the vocabulary of symbols that we might associate with the sacred will vary from person to person, depending not only on the religious myths and rituals each person is familiar with, but also on fundamental psychic associations based on experience. For example, if the first time someone told you about angels you were very young and at the time focusing on the brilliance of the speaker's red dress, the association of angels with the color red may well stick in your subconscious mind for life.

Tedlock tells of a sacred dream she had during the formative years of her shamanic training in which she encountered a dolphin wearing a diamond necklace while she was scuba diving in the Pacific Ocean. After discussing the dream with her teachers, she realized the dolphin was a sacred symbol for one of her deceased foremothers, who was trying to convey an important message to her. Unsure what that message was, she employed a Mayan practice known as "completing the dream," which, Tedlock writes "can allow one to learn to consciously enter into a dream."[17] The method involves focusing on a sacred symbol while crossing the threshold between waking and sleeping realms. She explains that this practice is similar to Jung's dream analysis, but Mayans perform their symbolic analysis while they are still dreaming. Once the dreamer has passed through the portal between waking and dreaming consciousness with the symbol still in mind, he can then amplify, move, or change the symbols in some way while dreaming.[18]

But completing the dream is a sacred practice that requires determination and patience. Tedlock notes that she had to work hard for 260 days until three dolphins reentered her dreams and she was able to work with them to figure out what sacred message her grandmother was trying to impart from the realm beyond the living. The dolphin became a sacred symbol for her, or, as her teacher explained it, her *nagual,* her messenger and destiny. Tedlock writes that she realized,

> Since dolphins are famous for their ability to navigate through the ocean by using sonar, emitting sounds and receiving back echoes, they seemed to be an auspicious symbol for my future practice of dream interpretation and divination.[19]

Tedlock believes that the Western cultural perspective on dreaming as "unreal" and waking experience as "real" limits the possible worlds and selves that can be represented in dreaming.[20] We must learn to free our thinking in this respect in order to develop continuity between waking and dreaming sacred consciousness in order to enhance our spiritual lives, and psychic sacred symbols are the portal between the two.

Slipping through the Portal between Sacred Waking Life Experiences and Sacred Dreams

1. Find your sacred dream symbol.

Think about dreams, visions, or experiences you have had that you believed were truly sacred. Do not worry if you cannot explain or do not completely understand why you believe they were sacred. Figuring that out is one of the main purposes of this practice. Think through these visions or experiences, looking for curious or recurring symbols. Writing in a journal everything you remember about them might be helpful, if you have not already done so. Remembering, keeping a journal about, and analyzing sacred dreams will be discussed in depth in part 3 of this book. But for now, although we are concerned with creating a continuum between sacred waking life experiences and sacred dreams for the

sake of spiritual self-understanding and growth, simply try to identify one or more symbols that seem to have presented themselves
to you as a means of sacred communication or understanding.

Any symbol you choose could be used as a continuum between waking and dreaming states of consciousness. Because
our main concern, however, is to explore the spiritual significance
of our dream consciousness so we can relate it to our waking
sacred awareness, you should have a good reason for choosing
a symbol you perceive as sacred. For example, I recommend you
not choose the image of a fox as a sacred symbol simply because
you have always thought foxes are mysterious and because you
were intrigued when you read in a book about animal symbolism that foxes are associated with shape-shifting. If, however, you
were once walking through the woods and had a face-to-face
encounter with a fox that seemed spiritually significant in a way
you could not put your finger on, that fox might be a good sacred
dream symbol for you. You can also draw upon previous dream
experiences for intriguing or odd sacred symbols to carry forward
into your waking-dreaming sacred consciousness, in the same
way Tedlock did in completing her dolphin dream.

Just as recurring dreams usually indicate that the unconscious
is desperately trying to convey something to the consciousness,
symbols that seem to recur in a sacred way in both waking life and
sleep can indicate that someone or something sacred is trying
to relate a spiritual message to you. To cite an example from my
personal experience, I recently led a spiritual retreat that opened
with the ritual act of creating an altar with items each participant
considered sacred. One woman pulled out a fluffy gray and white
bird's feather and shared that it was not at all what she had planned
to put on the altar, but it had fluttered down in front of her on her
way to our meeting, and she had suddenly gotten the feeling that
she should present it as her sacred offering. The day after I re-
turned home from the retreat, another participant contacted me,
relating that on her way home she stopped at one of the shrines

we had visited together. While she was praying, a feather fluttered down from the sky and landed in her hand. The following day I was saddened by the news that an acquaintance of mine had suddenly passed away. As I sat in my backyard offering up my prayer, the feather of a dove fluttered down, seemingly from nowhere, and landed at my feet. This series of fluttering feathers is not necessarily miraculous or supernatural. After all, it was the time of year when birds lose their feathers. However, the pattern of succession and the context within which each feather "presented itself" to each of us—who had recently been so connected in spirit—struck me as a message with sacred and profound meaning. Because I know that I still do not understand the true meaning of these occurrences, the sacred dream symbol I am now working with is the dove feather, the image frozen in my mind exactly as it lay on the ground in front of me.

Studies have shown that some people, especially those who are visually impaired, have dreams that are more auditory than visual. As evidenced by the use of the mantra *aum*, an auditory symbol, such as a locution (a voice calling your name or sacred message) or a phrase of music, can be an effective sacred dream symbol. Whether your symbol is visual or auditory, or takes some other form, however, you must place it in your mind with attention to every detail you remember about it when it presented itself to you. If you do not remember it perfectly, fill in the detail in your mind, but nurture a definite image or characteristic of your symbol in your consciousness. The reason for this specificity is that you will more easily keep your mind focused on it meditatively if it does not vary from one minute to the next or even from one sacred dream session to the next.

2. Practice "waking vision" meditation of your sacred dream symbol.

At least a couple of times a day, or more if your schedule permits, clear your mind of everything but your sacred dream symbol. You can do this anytime, anywhere, standing, sitting, or lying down, and some people can focus their minds meditatively enough to do this while walking. Wherever you are, straighten your spine. Breathe slowly but comfortably, and "hold" your sacred dream symbol in your mind. Do not try to manipulate or analyze it in any way. Just let it be itself while enveloping all levels of your consciousness. If other thoughts interfere, do as many ancient meditative techniques instruct and watch them float over your mind like a cloud. But watch that cloud float behind your sacred dream symbol. Continue this exercise for at least a few minutes, but longer if possible.

3. Perform presleep sacred dream rituals.

Looking back at the predream rituals discussed in chapter 1 for the practice of incubating sacred dreams, perform the ones that seem to work best for you. Whether you take a ritual bath, light a candle, chant, sing, or dance, do whatever you need to do to assure your psyche you are transitioning from your waking life routine into sacred dreamtime. If your symbol is something you can put close to your bed or under your pillow, like my feather, do so. If not, you might choose to draw, paint, or sculpt it. All that is really necessary for this practice, though, is to enter your sacred sleep space with a definite mental image of the symbol.

4. Practice presleep sacred symbol meditation.

When you retire, lie in a comfortable position—preferably on your back, because you will more easily be able to extend your spine, which is important for meditative breathing. Take a deep, comfortable breath and feel it filling your whole body with soft, bright light. Hold the breath momentarily before exhaling slowly. Breathe in this manner as you continue to visualize your sacred dream symbol exactly as you did in your waking dream sacred symbol meditation. If you feel the urge to roll over, do so, but continue to focus on your sacred dream symbol until you fall asleep.

5. Slip through the portal between waking sacred vision and sacred dreaming.

With continued practice, you will find that at times you are able to carry your sacred symbol concentration through the stages of hypnagogia and into the first stage of REM sleep, when you can often feel the presence or character of your sacred symbol, even if you cannot visualize it. Usually this stage passes relatively quickly into the second stage, but often, while you cycle through the second through fourth stages of sleep where dreaming slows down and stops, your unconscious fertilizes the meaning of the symbol. By the time you cycle back to the longer period of REM sleep, your dreams may come alive with new dimensions and deeper meanings of the symbol. Be aware throughout this process that dreams consist of systems of symbols. Your sacred symbol dreaming may well open the way to a host of related symbols that can help you understanding the sacred nature of your dreaming. Write down whatever you can remember upon waking. Details are important, even if they seem irrelevant at first.

Part Two

Dreaming as a Sacred Experience

CHAPTER THREE

MYSTICAL DREAMING

Today sacred dreams are often referred to as mystical dreams. The word "mystic" implies mystery and wonder, and the practice known in the West as "mysticism" involves spiritual union or special communication with the Divine. As noted earlier, though mystical dreaming has been practiced by spiritual adepts throughout the ages all over the world, Westerners' ability to embrace the practice has been thwarted by a perception that it is unreal or unimportant because it cannot be studied under a microscope or even using an EEG machine. Nonetheless, mystical dreaming is a reality for at least half the world's population and a vital part of personal understanding and growth—not only spiritually, but mentally and emotionally as well. Thus, we must find means for identifying the true nature of mystical dreams, learn to navigate the sleeping consciousness gracefully and peacefully through them, and accept the gifts and fruits they bring.

One of the few contemporary studies on mystical dreaming is Bulkeley's interviews with one hundred participants on their sleep and dream patterns in relation to family life, religious beliefs, and political attitudes. As noted earlier, Bulkeley found that, generally speaking, the participants described their most memorable dreams as mystical. He concluded:

Mystical dreams are experienced by around half the population and by women more than men, and their prototypical form involves good fortunes, friendly interactions, and unusual or nonhuman characters.[1]

Bulkeley also noted that the participants experienced certain motifs, including recurring mystical dream settings and situations. Listed in the order of the frequency with which they were reported, they include death or visitations from deceased loved ones, encounters with religious figures (including figures of God, Jesus, Mary, and angels), brilliant light, precognition, reassurance, nightmares, and epistemological confusion (most notably the blurring of the boundary between the sleeping dream and a waking experience). A few participants also said they were aware that they had had a significant mystical dream that they could not remember. Though, as Bulkeley says, the sample of his study was too small to allow sweeping generalizations about how most people experience mystical dreams, I find the motifs he identified are consistent with those of the mystical dreamers I have worked with. For this reason, I believe we would benefit by taking a closer look at each one.

MYSTICAL DREAMS OF VISITATIONS AND DEATH

At first glance, we might see irony in Bulkeley's finding that although mystical dreams were generally characterized as experiences of good fortune and friendly interactions and that they involved unusual characters, the most common motif was death. The mystical or mysterious nature of these dreams associates them with the unknown, however, in a manner that is more intriguing than dreadful. The greatest psychological "unknown" humans grapple with, consciously and unconsciously, is death. This sacred dream motif also makes sense when we consider that perhaps the main function of religious systems and spiritual quests is to answer the great yet basic philosophical questions of life such as, "Who am I?" "Why am I here?" "Who made me and why?" And most important, "What happens to me and my loved ones after we die?" Dreams of visitations from loved ones who have gone before us and dreams in which we die provide answers to these questions and consequently are of monumental sacred importance.

Visitation dreams are extremely common. Not only do they provide consolation that our deceased loved ones are all right, but they give the deceased a voice with which they can offer us advice for our present lives and relationships, and hopeful glimpses into life beyond our own physical death. In Western culture these dreams are usually regarded as merely part of the human psyche's attempt to deal with grief. I believe, however, that we can learn much about visitation dreams from cultures in which the sacred connection with deceased ancestors is understood as a dynamic reality. As a consistent dreamer of sacred visitation dreams, I can attest that these dreams are so charged with power and spiritual impact that they impress me as much as any waking life experience I have ever had. Because of the restrictions most of us have unwittingly placed on our waking consciousness, the sleeping dream is the most accessible place for the souls of the departed to communicate with us.

A few years ago, I experienced multiple dreams about a man I had been deeply and romantically involved with when I was much younger. We had lost contact with one another long before, and I had not given the relationship much thought in quite a while. Our encounters within the dream were amicable, peaceful, and profoundly real. I believe it is no coincidence that I later found out he had died just about the time the dreams occurred. In my mind he was reaching out to me from a spirit world beyond my immediate understanding. He needed closure, and the sacred dreamscape was the place where he knew he could make it happen.

As macabre as dreams of death—especially your own— might appear to be, dream psychologists are united in asserting that, once analyzed, most death dreams seem to serve as metaphors for transformations from one stage or situation in life to another, rather than as an indication or prophecy of anyone's physical death. Sleep and dream experts also agree that dreams themselves are virtually harmless. Stories that have circulated about dying as a result of a dream, perhaps from hitting the ground while dreaming that you are falling, are completely superstitious. If you do not awaken during the fall, dream researchers say, you will usually land surprisingly lightly.

Remembering that dreams are largely metaphorical in nature, we can deduce that a dream in which you experience yourself as dying would signify the death of an aspect of self, like the loss we experience in the move from adolescence to adulthood, from student to career seeker, or even from single life to married life or parenthood. It also signals a new way of life, however. We need to recognize that dreams of death are sacred metaphors for life transformations in the same spiritual sense that we see death as an integral aspect of resurrection or rebirth into a new and usually better way of living. We should also note that the mystical dreams Bulkeley classified as those of "reassurance" included dreams of death because the dreamers associated them with comfort, consolation, and relief from suffering.

MYSTICAL DREAM ENCOUNTERS WITH RELIGIOUS FIGURES

The second most common mystical dreams remembered by the participants in Bulkeley's study featured "direct references to Christianity, including the figures of God, Jesus, Mary, and angels."[2] Christian references were frequent because over half the people he interviewed identified themselves as Christians, and a majority of them were Roman Catholic. The religious views of the study group would also explain why one recurring mystical theme included radiant visions of Mary. Obviously, non-Christian sacred dreamers encounter images of religious figures or conceptions of Ultimate Reality from their own religious traditions or personal belief systems.

This type of mystical dream—a visitation and interaction with the image of a sacred figure from our religious tradition with whom we strongly identify—is the one most of us probably expect to have when cultivating a sacred dream. Bulkeley also noted that although most of these dreams expressed positive attitudes about Christianity, a few involved darker themes, such as Satan and Christ doing battle, the apocalypse, and God's judgment. Dreamers also identified a few of these dreams as a form of revelation.

These dreams are the ones in which the cultural religious stories and myths with which we are most accustomed will play themselves out in our psyches. This is not to say that they are merely psychical constructs or simply dreams of sacred "wish fulfillment," as Freud described psychological dreaming, or even the opposite—our deepest fears playing themselves out. Though I believe both types of dreams do occur, I would not be quick to dismiss on either basis the importance of the presence of the sacred religious figure. From my experience, more often than not the sacred dream figure seems to come to the dreamer to impart a message of particular sacred significance.

MYSTICAL DREAMS OF LIGHT

A profusion of light is a frequent motif of sacred dreams. Usually even sacred dreams of death involve a dynamic interplay of light, and sacred religious figures are usually surrounded by a halo of light, just as they often are in religious iconography. The

art of Tibetan dream yoga includes visualization of a sophisticated system of colored lights that, according to Buddhist
beliefs, correspond to the lights the spirit of a person encounters
after death. Learning to navigate the self toward the right lights
in the dreamscape prepares you to navigate through the liminal
realm between lives toward a desirable rebirth.

White, clear, or opalescent light is a common metaphor
for Divine Reality in dreams and in religious mythological
and ritual systems, probably because it symbolizes the ability
to "see"—literally and figuratively. I believe it signifies what
is known as the "noetic" nature of sacred dreaming. From the
Greek term *noesis,* meaning cognitive thought, noetic communion or communication with the Divine has been sought
in hopes of acquiring spiritual wisdom—esoteric knowledge
or revelation that contains answers to the great philosophical
questions of life.

Of course, basic human experience with the workings of the
cosmos suggests that the Divine is composed of or surrounded
by light. Observation of the natural cycle of life—the depend-
able passing of the nurturing sun and the nightly phases of the
moon, which somehow magically turn the tides and regulate
the regenerative flow of the human biological birthing process—has resulted in numerous myths that equate the sun and
moon with deities. The ethereal luminescence, movement, and
spacing of the stars have prompted humankind to assume these
heavenly bodies have divine attributes.

Perhaps, however, the most important reason that Ultimate
Reality often appears surrounded by light in dreams is that
the light protects the mysterious spiritual essence of Ultimate
Reality. Even religions that view the Divine as a god or goddess
in day-to-day prayer and ritual usually adhere to the belief that
he, she, or it is essentially spirit and therefore not subject to the
confines of the human biological body. Intense light diminishes

the tendency to experience Divine Reality as an embodied male or female human and preserves the otherworldly wonder we long to experience in our sacred dreams. Light can be ambiguous like other common dream symbols, such as fire or serpents: light not only brightens and reveals, but, if it is bright enough—as it often is in dreams—it blinds.

I am not suggesting that dreams in which the Divine is experienced as light are not genuine sacred dreams or even that what is experienced as light is not the Divine. I am saying, however, that the Divine comes to us in dreams in the metaphorical constructs we can most readily respond to, based on our personal and cultural experience of the Sacred.

MYSTICAL DREAMS OF PROPHECY

The prophetic nature of mystical dreams is well documented in the scriptures of the world's religions, and this is reflected in Bulkeley's study as well. Several of the participants he interviewed remembered narrative dreams that foretold a future event of great significance to the dreamer. Referring to these as precognitive dreams, Bulkeley further notes that these dreams were described by the dreamers in his study as spiritual intuitions of the future and highly valued as such.[3]

The history of the world has been shaped by sacred prophetic dreams. Roman Emperor Constantine dreamed Jesus came to him and told him to place the Greek insignia for Christ on the shields of his soldiers as he went into the final battle to gain control of the empire. Constantine did so, and after he won the battle against Maxentius at the Milvian Bridge in 312 CE, he legalized Christianity and dramatically changed the character of the religion. The angel Gabriel appeared to Muhammad in a dreamlike vision and instructed him to leave the city of Medina, where the message of the Qur'an was not originally well received. In the dream he was encouraged to move to

Mecca, where Islam took root and quickly spread. Years after Harriet Tubman led nineteen Underground Railroad trips that freed more than 300 slaves, she explained that sacred dreams helped her to find the safe pathways. She never lost a single "passenger." These are but a few of the many accounts of sacred dreams that shaped human history, but they are good examples of how important sacred prophetic dreams are. We must wonder how different the world would be today if any of these prophetic dreams had not occurred or if the dreamers had not taken them seriously.

MYSTICAL NIGHTMARES

Just as the frequency of death's appearance in dreams might seem ironic, we might view as paradoxical Bulkeley's finding that eight of the one hundred dreams described as mystical in his study were also experienced as nightmares. These dreams included fighting, chasing, struggling, dangers, and misfortunes. The reason Bulkeley believed them to be mystical was that religious imagery played a role in the conflict. The most evident reason for this pairing is that in religious belief systems that are traditionally dualistic, such as Christianity, religious good is historically, mythologically, and psychically balanced with forces of evil. The writings of Christian mystics are fraught with accounts of Satan or satanic demons intervening in their mystical union with God or Christ through a variety of tricks and temptations. This religious imagery is bound to carry over into sacred dreams.

On several occasions when I tried to cultivate a sacred dream, I was shocked to fall straight into a nightmare instead. I have since learned to control this phenomenon by developing my ability to experience these dreams with lucidity and to redirect a troubling dream. (I discuss this method in depth in the following chapter.) Because I was raised with a traditional

Roman Catholic understanding of the Sacred, this redirection of my sacred intention to the realm of the profane may well have been at work. At a deeper level of the psyche, however, I believe more is at play in this phenomenon. For the soul, a journey toward union with the Sacred is of such monumental importance that it becomes, as dreams often do, a highly emotional endeavor. Once human emotions are triggered, they can flow in just about any direction—especially in dreams, when we are shifted into deeper levels of consciousness.

I have learned in years of researching and teaching about the religions of the world that no matter how devoutly we believe in the presence and power of what we perceive as sacred, we often experience a psychological undercurrent of "What if ... ?" Anyone who has ever truly thought through his religious beliefs has grappled with the question, "What if what I have been holding as divine or sacred reality doesn't exist? What if it is not of the nature I have always assumed?" Such questions are a healthy way of examining religious affiliation and convictions and are usually fleeting emotional responses to the ongoing development of a mature religious identity. These are the sorts of issues, however, that even if we have long since worked through them on a conscious level, still lurk in the unconscious. As we cycle through the stages of sleep and deep-dream consciousness, sacred dreams we have cultivated or that occur on their own may from time to time trigger these latent anxieties. In developing methods of dreaming as a sacred art, we should be aware of the possibility of mystical nightmares. If you have already had a number of sacred dream experiences, you have probably had an anxiety-filled dream. Because these dreams are relatively rare, however—and for most sacred dreamers who practice methods of lucidity, they are also controllable—I would encourage you not to allow them to inhibit your progress in the art of sacred dreaming.

OTHER CHARACTERISTICS OF
MYSTICAL DREAMS

Other mystical dreams Bulkeley identified were characterized by epistemological confusion or made a sacred impact but left the dreamer with no actual memory of the dream itself. Their significance lay in the dreamers' responses to or thoughts about the dream. Although I think of motifs as symbols or symbol systems that arise from the content of the dream, both of these mystical dream phenomena are worthy of further consideration, because they help to distinguish the mystical dream experience from other dreams.

What Bulkeley is referring to as "epistemological confusion" is a mystical dream with such intense mental, emotional, sensual, and often physical impact that the dreamer awakens sensing that the dream was more like profound experiences in waking life than previous dreams. As a result, a sense of confusion or disorientation about the dream and its significance ensues. For example, many people have reported mystical dreams of visitation from deceased loved ones, like the one I shared earlier, and in most cases, they have been left with the lasting conviction, as I was, that that person visited them in reality and not just within the dream.

Usually after the dreamer awakens, any dream that is remembered begins to dim and the dreamer quickly becomes aware that any traces of the action or narrative that remain in his consciousness were those of a sleeping dream. This phenomenon rarely occurs in mystical dreams. Upon awakening the dreamer will either remember the dream with such vivid imagery and emotion that she will not be able to differentiate the experience from a waking life experience, or she will not remember the actual dream at all, but will be charged with awareness that something so profoundly sacred has taken place that it has significantly changed her life.

To explain this in another manner, our psychic consciousness responds to both external and internal stimuli. Those
of us who have been conditioned by the traditional Western
understanding of consciousness tend to accept the view that in
waking life we respond primarily to external stimuli—that is,
events, ideas, and sensory input (visual, auditory, tactile, and so
forth) from daily life. Once we experience this external input,
it becomes a matter of internal consciousness. We consciously
process a certain amount of it, but most of it passes directly into
our unconscious. As Jung explained, the data that has been
internalized by different levels of consciousness speaks to us
during our dreams. Ideas we consciously considered for various
reasons during waking life the previous few days often influence lighter stages of sleep and dream experience, while concepts or concerns we have repressed in deeper levels of internal
consciousness might attempt to command our attention in
deeper or later stages of REM dream sleep. But what if, as many
dreamers of non-Western cultures have insisted, we can access
external events in dreams?

One way of looking at this possibility is through a model
of the four levels or dimensions of consciousness explained
by clinical psychologist Stephen Aizenstat, who developed a
method of dream work he calls "dream tending." In a form
similar to the Mandukya Upanishad, he presents the first level
of the psyche as that of everyday experience. The second level,
the personal unconscious, he describes as a repository of experiences or memories that shape human personal characteristics.
Aizenstat believes that the collective unconscious of archetypes,
as described by Jung, constitutes a third dimension of consciousness, where we can enter the realm of shared human experience as expressed in the mythological symbolism of the ancient
world, which lives on in fairy tales, folklore, literature, and the-
ater. The fourth level he calls the "world consciousness" or the

"ecological consciousness." Aizenstat asserts that on this level, the human psyche lives inside an extended world consciousness where the psychic phenomena of the world—not just its people, but also rocks, mountains, oceans, in fact, all created of reality—can enter into the dreams of people.[4]

Aizenstat says that a dream can draw on one or more levels or even from realms between levels. For example, it might incorporate images from experiences the dreamer had in the previous day or two during waking life consciousness with symbols from the collective conscious. But his understanding that, on the fourth level, the human psyche is able to enter into a world consciousness at large offers the attractive possibility that the human psyche can experience input from external sources while dreaming. Aizenstat's focus is not on the sacred nature or possibilities of the dream. But if his model of the levels of the psyche is correct, those of us who experience the natural world as a sacred realm created by and imbued with Divine Reality could certainly experience on this level of consciousness a mystical dream reality that had not entered the psyche during waking life experiences.

In analyzing all the data he gleaned about mystical dreams from his interviews, Bulkeley observed that

> the mystical dreams reported by these participants were filled with strange, supernatural, counterfactual phenomena. By any measure, they are quite bizarre dreams. They are not, however, disjointed, vague, fragmented or jumbled. On the contrary, they display remarkable coherence, vividness, and realism, more it seems than is found in ordinary dreams.[5]

He went on note that participants in this study who experienced dreams they considered mystical also experienced them with a sense of reality that was surprisingly consistent with the individual's waking life experiences.[6]

Evaluating my own sacred dream experience and that of people who have shared theirs with me, I believe that humans possess the ability to access external sacred reality on a deep level of dream consciousness and that many people do. The mystical dream impresses us with profound reality—whether we remember it or not—because it is real and involves every aspect of our conscious and unconscious being. But it happens in such a deep state of consciousness that if it does not imprint itself deeply on the personal consciousness, we may not remember its details. One of the reasons we might not remember the mystical dream itself upon awakening is that the dreamer may have entered the sacred realm so completely as to bypass the usual reliance on everyday consciousness imagery. In this case, the waking life memories of the dream would have no means with which to "see" it. Another reason might be that the content of the dream may not have been as important for the dreamer as knowledge of the sacred experience itself. Those who do awaken remembering the mystical dream itself, however, tend to be so impressed with its impact that they never forget it.

Recognizing and Responding to the Sacred Dream Presence

Someone who feels she has experienced a mystical dream will need no proof that it was such and will be confident that the dream has conveyed as much profound truth as any experience she might have had in waking life. But dreamers commonly have difficulty articulating their experience of the mystical or sacred presence of the dream. For this reason, even though the dreamer usually feels compelled to respond to the dream in some way, he can be confused about how to do so. The purpose of this practice is to recognize the character of the sacred dream presence and to discern what can be learned from the mystical dream experience and how to respond to it.

I have adapted this exercise from "Existential Dream Practice," a method of examining dream content in *Integral Dreaming: A Holistic Approach to Dreams* by dream researchers Fariba Bogzaran and Daniel Deslauriers.[7] I was introduced to this practice in a graduate class on dreaming I took with Deslauriers. By working with a partner on the phone, I learned through this method to unlock the mysteries about a character in one of my most memorable mystical dreams, opening my sense of spiritual self and spiritual dreaming self to new dimensions of meaning and significance. Because I do not want my experience with this practice to inadvertently color yours, I will not share the details of my experience here.

1. Enlist the help of a dream listener.

Anyone you feel you can trust to honor your work with your sacred dreams and with whom you do not mind sharing some of the workings of your innermost consciousness will be fine. But working with someone who is on a similar quest or who is at least willing to explore the dimensions of her own sacred dream consciousness is especially rewarding. In that case, after you have completed the practice, you can switch roles and listen to your partner's sacred dream presence work.

2. Select a dream you have had that you believe had sacred or mystical significance.

If you have had more than one such dream, select the one that is the most memorable or one that has recurred. Thinking through the narrative of the dream, select and focus on the presence in the dream that seemed to be charged with sacred energy. This presence may have manifested itself as a deity, a person, an animal, an object, or any natural feature of the dreamscape, such as light, water, sand, and the like. As we have seen, dreams often present their significance through symbolic metaphor, so anything you may have felt had sacred meaning is suitable for this exercise. If you have more than one sacred dream presence in mind, I suggest you select the one that seems most curious or oddest to you or one that recurs with the most frequency in your dreams.

3. **Briefly describe to your listener aspects of the dream that involve the sacred presence.**

You do not need to reconstruct the entire narrative of the dream. Sometimes the important aspects of dream symbolism manifest themselves more readily when taken out of the context of the dream.

4. **Close your eyes and visualize the sacred presence as it appeared in your dream.**

After a minute or so, the listener softly asks, "Who are you?" The dreamer spontaneously shares what comes to her mind. When the dreamer comes to a natural break in describing who her dream presence is, the listener asks again, "Who are you?" The dreamer again spontaneously shares whatever occurs to her. The listener and dreamer continue this process for as long as it is fruitful for the dreamer. Usually, the first round of the dreamer's answers will consist of a description of the image, and each successive round will contain a deeper awareness of what the mystical dream presence signified or was trying to convey to the dreamer.

5. **Immediately after completing the practice, write in your journal what you have learned about your sacred dream presence.**

Be sure to write your overall feelings, ideas, and conclusions, as well as any details that might have come up. By this time you should have at least a general idea of the significance of the sacred dream presence and what it was trying to convey to you. If not, increasing your awareness of what you have learned in this exercise during waking and sleeping consciousness should eventually make the intentions of the sacred presence clear.

6. Respond to the sacred dream presence in whatever manner seems appropriate.

The response could be something as simple as determining to remain aware of a sacred reality, saying a prayer, offering forgiveness, or making a phone call. It might involve a greater endeavor, such as executing a sacred work of art or even embarking on a new spiritual vocation or form of activism. The important thing is that as soon as you feel that you are beginning to understand what message the sacred presence was conveying to you, you act on it, at least in some small way. By responding to the sacred dream image, you enter into relationship with it. This not only sanctions the mystical dream encounter and offers gratitude for its sacred gifts, but enhances your ability to experience and enjoy future sacred dreams and new dimensions of spiritual growth and fulfillment.

CHAPTER FOUR

LUCID DREAMING AS A SACRED ART

The best way to navigate through the sacred dreamscape is in a state of lucidity. If you know you are dreaming, you can reflect on sacred dream content while dreaming. And even more important, if you are confronted with a dream presence, you can immediately interact with it and perhaps even discern the spiritual significance of the dream before you wake up. Though some people seem to be more naturally prone to lucid dreaming, with practice and patience just about anyone can master the art and develop it into a routine aspect of their spirituality with exhilarating results and endless possibilities.

Stories of sacred lucid dreaming from the world's religions abound. For centuries, shamans of many indigenous cultures have guided the souls of the departed into the land of the dead in lucid dreams, and Native Americans still rely on conscious dreaming for their vision quests.[1] The Muslim Sufi mystics have traditionally used lucid dreaming as a means of achieving ecstatic union with Allah. And the twelfth-century Christian mystic Hildegard of Bingen documented her frequent lucid dream encounters with God, who appeared to her in the form of a mandala (or circle) of sacred energy.

By far the most sophisticated philosophy of lucid dreaming as a spiritual practice has been developed by the Tibetan Bön Buddhist tradition. As previously mentioned, the purpose of the sacred lucid dream discipline, or yoga, taught by the Tibetan masters is to train the consciousness to direct itself through the liminal realm that it will encounter after physical death. Because going to sleep is like dying in the sense that it is a journey into the unknown, followers of the Tibetan tradition believe a proficient lucid dreamer will be prepared to navigate his consciousness through the *bardo*, the liminality of the afterlife, and into a desirable rebirth. According to the Tibetan masters, one who has perfected spiritual lucid dream techniques will be able to pass out of the *bardo* and enter the clear light of liberation from the cycle of rebirth.

Aside from the Tibetan Bön tradition, the other comprehensive method of lucid dream practice is that of the famous dream psychologist Stephen LaBerge. In the late 1970s he proved lucid dreaming is a real phenomenon to the satisfaction of Western scientific thinkers by performing prearranged eye movements during REM sleep in a laboratory. When the EEG registered the uncharacteristic left-to-right pattern at one- to two-minute intervals, researchers concluded LaBerge was cognizant of the fact that he was asleep and dreaming, and was able to carry out a dream task that he had intended before he went to sleep. LaBerge went on to devote his career to the study of lucid dreaming. Drawing to some extent on the ancient Tibetan lucid dream yoga, he developed several techniques to help dreamers enter lucid dream states and navigate themselves successfully and joyfully through them.

By comparing and contrasting the Tibetan Bön masters' spiritual approach to lucid dreaming to the more scientific approach of LaBerge (whose focus is not on the sacred nature of dreaming), some useful methods of cultivating and navigating through lucid dreams can be gleaned for those who wish to develop the art of sacred dreaming. In this chapter I lean on the wisdom of both of these sources to suggest ways you can learn to engage in lucid dreams as a regular spiritual practice, and I propose methods of navigating through them that will enrich personal spiritual wisdom and growth.

DEVELOPING THE ABILITY TO ENGAGE IN SACRED LUCID DREAMS

Regardless of whether you have already had some lucid dream experience, according to studies conducted by LaBerge, just about anyone who is willing to make the effort can cultivate the ability to regularly experience lucid dreams. The lucid dream world can be somewhat unpredictable at first, however, so only someone who is already fairly well in tune with his dream pattern should purposely venture into it. In a book he coauthored with media specialist Howard Rheingold, *Exploring the World of Lucid Dreaming,* LaBerge suggests that you should be able to remember at least one dream per night before attempting lucid dream induction techniques.[2] Chances are that by reading this book and doing some of the previous dream practices, you are already at this level, and I hope you are also aware that you have had one or more sacred dreams.

Because lucid dreaming is essentially the state of being aware of the fact you are dreaming, the best way to reach this awareness is to ask yourself whether you are dreaming while you are still dreaming. The most effective way to train yourself to ask this question during a sleeping dream is to regularly do it while you are awake. LaBerge and Rheingold recommend asking the question, "Am I dreaming or am I awake right now?" at least five to ten times during the day. They say you should not immediately declare yourself awake, for if you develop that habit, you will do the same thing while dreaming. They suggest different ways to do a reality check to see whether you are dreaming that you could do even when you are not asleep. Look around your dreamscape for oddities or inconsistencies— things that are obviously out of place or unnatural. For example, they advise you to look around for something in writing. Read it if you can, look away, and then read it again. LaBerge and Rheingold say every time they try this in a dream, the writing seems to mutate before the second reading. They also say looking at a digital clock or watch is an effective test, because they never seem to behave correctly in dreams. Think back over what has transpired in the last few minutes; if you have trouble remembering, you might be dreaming.[3]

The practice of training the mind for lucid dreaming during the day is framed a little differently in the Tibetan Buddhist tradition. As we have seen, waking life experience is thought to be the same as dream experience, because both are seen as projections of the mind resulting from karma, or what is wrought by past experience and action. Therefore, Tenzin Rinpoche suggests that simply reminding yourself throughout the day that you are dreaming will help prompt the dreaming mind to do the same, which should ultimately prompt the lucid dream state during sleep. "Throughout the day," Tenzin Rinpoche says, "practice the recognition of the dream-like nature of life until the same recognition begins to manifest in dream."[4] He gives practical suggestions on how this should be done:

> Upon waking in the morning, think to yourself, "I am awake in a dream." When you walk into the kitchen, recognize it as a dream kitchen. Pour dream milk into dream coffee. "It's all a dream," you think to yourself, "this is a dream." Remind yourself of this constantly throughout the day.[5]

Tenzin Rinpoche says that throughout the practice of experiencing waking life as a dream, keeping the focus on yourself as a dreamer rather than on the events of the dream is important. He suggests you imagine yourself as an illusion, a dream figure, in a body that is not solid. If you can master this technique until you remain in this awareness, Tenzin Rinpoche maintains, you will experience greater lucidity not only while dreaming, but also while awake.

LaBerge and Rheingold developed a method for prompting the consciousness to ask itself if it is asleep while it actually is sleeping. They suggest we should train our minds to look for what he calls "dreamsigns," which can be like neon lights flashing in the darkness signaling, "This is a dream!" Dreamsigns can be anything in the dream that seems bizarre or out of place—words that mutate, fickle digital clocks, or, as in one dream example he used, obviously out of place cobblestones in an otherwise realistic scene. If you train your mind to watch for such odd occurrences while awake, they are more likely to trigger lucidity while dreaming. Another method of using dreamsigns to flip the consciousness switch to awareness is to recognize recurring patterns or symbols in your dreams and train the psyche to recognize those in future dreams. Sacred dream symbols that you may have developed into regular dream patterns from the sacred dream practice in chapter 2 can become particularly potent sacred dreamsigns.

I became adept at lucid dreaming by using the dreamsign method during the year following the death of my sister. She came to me frequently in dreams, so before I went to sleep every night, I vowed that when I encountered her in a dream, I would realize I was dreaming, so I could talk to her. The technique worked with amazing regularity, and since then, even without the prompt, I experience lucid dreams at a much higher rate. Once the consciousness is trained to recognize it is dreaming, the door is flung open to the infinite and amazing world of sacred dreaming.

NAVIGATING THROUGH SACRED LUCID DREAMS

Once you have entered a state of lucidity, you can train your dreaming mind to do just about anything you want it to. After I routinely entered lucidity in dreams where I encountered my sister, I started to program my dream mind so when I saw her in future dreams I would fly. It worked perfectly. She visited me in my bedroom, and after a lovely talk, I excused myself and took off. I enjoyed lucid dreamflight so much that in subsequent months, as soon as I become aware that I was dreaming, I instantaneously became airborne.

Frequent lucid dreamers consistently report that their senses are heightened in this state, to the point that their experiences are richer, broader, deeper, and more pleasurable than in waking life. Lucid dreams are often characterized by brilliant light or colors, intense emotions, and a sense of liberation or exhilaration.[6] Because of this phenomenon, coupled with the fact that the sleeping consciousness is more apt to allow us to participate in activities that are taboo in waking consciousness, some people have admitted they are addicted to lucid dream acts of power and sex, and an endless array of base behaviors of personal wish fulfillment. With the spiritual dreamers I have worked with, I have found that once they become adept at lucid dreaming, they often play around with the sensational aspects of it but quickly become bored and shift their endeavors to experience the sacred benefits of lucidity. Proficient lucid dreamers are free to explore their own horizons, but those who use them as a sacred art are particularly well rewarded with great joy, bliss, and ecstasy.

Some dream researchers and lucid dream adepts believe the dreamer should passively allow the events of a lucid dream to unfold, rather than trying to control the action of the dream. In the case of spiritual dreaming, I agree that in some dreams, especially those that involve a sense of a sacred presence that has come to impart an important message, taking a more receptive role can be more productive. In these cases, a lucid dreamer with spiritual sensibilities would probably understand this and respond accordingly. For the majority of mystical dreams, however, I tend to take the same stance as Tenzin Rinpoche, who claims that "it is better for the lucid and aware dreamer to control the dream than for the dreamer to be dreamed."[7] Even in sacred message dreams, the ability to lucidly converse with or respond to the sacred presence within the dream will usually enhance the sacred dreaming experience and exponentially increase the benefits that can be derived from it. Herein lies the true art of sacred lucid dreaming.

LaBerge and Rheingold see dreams as simulations of the world created by our perceptual systems. In other words, what we perceive as reality in dreams is, in their estimation, created by our conscious experience and remembered sensations. For this reason, the core of their advice on navigation through the dreamscape in a state of lucidity is that you should fully enjoy the sensual and perceptual wish-fulfillment dimensions of whatever activities present themselves or can be induced by the dreamer. They share the testimonies of several lucid dreamers who have done so in a variety of ways.

They do describe some useful lucid dream techniques for steering the consciousness around some of the troubling experiences that sometimes accompany lucid sacred dreams, including nightmares and the sleep paralysis that often results in what have become known as night terrors. If you know you are dreaming during a nightmare, LaBerge and Rheingold affirm that you can often change the dream scene by consciously trying to spread your arms and spin around like a top. They say this technique also works when trying to avoid waking from a good lucid dream that begins to fade.

Monsters, intruders, or any presence that seems threatening within a dream can usually be disarmed or dismissed with amazing ease in lucid dreams. Dream psychologists tend to agree that running from aggressors or trying to forcibly overtake them in dreams tends only to encourage them to come back in future dreams. The reason for this reappearance is that the unconscious fear of whatever a monster symbolizes to the dreamer has not been dealt with on the conscious level. Modern psychological analysis of such dreams shows that if the motives of the monster or aggressor are examined, the unconscious problem or threat becomes clear. Then the dreamer can usually not only disempower the dream foe, but obtain personal healing and growth. The lucid dreamer can do all of this within the dream itself. In most cases, if the dreamer stands his ground in the dream while the aggressor advances, the aggressor fades in potency. If it does not disappear, the dreamer can simply ask the dream intruder what it wants. More often than not, the answer will be surprisingly simple and remarkably healing for the waking consciousness as well.

Sleep paralysis is a phenomenon that affects many people within sacred lucid dreaming. This probably occurs because, as the mind starts to awaken, the body can still remain in the state of paralysis from deep REM sleep, when lucid dreaming is most active. Because the consciousness is in the liminal state between dreaming and wakefulness, the dreamer may experience hallucinations, including incredibly loud and realistic noises; the sensation of being approached, touched, or held down by a threatening figure; vibrations or the sensation of electricity running through the body; or the feeling of distortions of the body, being oppressed by a great weight, or difficulty breathing. Sometimes the dreamer has the sensation of leaving his body by floating up, sinking down through the bed, or a "false awakening," thinking he is arising and going about his daily business while his body is still asleep in bed.

I believe that the strange in-between quality of consciousness during sleep paralysis lends itself to dreaming that is also experienced as sacred or mystical, in that both are associated with the sensation of being between worlds or states of reality. The hallucinations that often accompany sleep paralysis during dreams that are perceived as sacred have historically given rise to mythological dream fears of visitations by devils, demons, incubi, or succubi. The initial response of the dreamer is to cry out for help or attempt to wake the body up, which usually results in a traumatic struggle before waking in a pool of sweat, feeling more drained and exhausted than you would if you had not slept at all.

LaBerge and Rheingold offer wonderful advice to the lucid sufferer of night terrors. First, they recommend that, as the dreamer, you remember that you are dreaming and therefore the experience is harmless, and second, relax and go with it. They suggest you adopt an attitude of curiosity, for dreams that proceed from paralysis experiences are often quite intense and wonderful.[8] The real gift of the dark cloud that enshrouds night terrors for those who tend to experience them regularly is that they can be wonderful dreamsigns with which the dreamer can enter a state of lucidity. Because night terrors happen when the consciousness is in the realm between REM sleep and waking, it is particularly receptive to returning to lucid dream activity. If you are prone to having night terrors, before going to sleep, set the dream intention that once you begin experiencing one, you will realize you are dreaming and redirect your consciousness to a more satisfying sacred dream experience.

For all of LaBerge's research on the psychological aspects of lucid dreaming and how to manipulate the lucid dreaming process, his focus is not on navigation through the spiritual aspects of lucid dreaming, nor is it featured in the study on lucid dream exploration he wrote with Rheingold. For this, we must turn to the Tibetan Bön tradition.

THE TIBETAN BÖN METHOD OF NAVIGATING THROUGH SACRED LUCID DREAMS

The Tibetan Bön method or yoga of spiritual dreaming is based on techniques for controlling the subtle psychic *prana,* or energy, that is believed to underlie human wisdom and emotion. For sacred dreaming, this involves meditative breathing that activates three root channels of energy in the body that are aligned with the psychic energy centers, or chakras. The white channel is the conduit of negative human energy and emotions, the red channel carries wisdom and positive emotions, and the blue channel is where primordial energy and nonduality reside. The blue channel is located in the center and aligns with the spine. The red and white channels run parallel on either side—the white on the right and red on the left for men; and for women, the opposite.

Lucidity itself is not the goal of Tibetan sacred dream yoga. It is a tool used to aid the process in order to reach the primary goal of Tibetan Buddhism, to free the self from the cycle of rebirth. Because this is not necessarily the goal for many sacred dreamers, I will not offer a comprehensive explanation of the method of activating the chakras and centering the dream energy in the central blue channel. For this I refer the reader to Tenzin Rinpoche's *The Tibetan Yogas of Dream and Sleep.* However, I mention it here because I think we need to understand that in the Tibetan Bön tradition, dreaming is understood as a psychosomatic process. Sacred lucid dreaming begins with a highly ritualized awareness of the energy in the physical body and its quality as emotionally good or bad, and it requires activating and balancing this energy through breath control before entering the sleeping dream state. The idea is that this energy carries over into the sleeping-dreaming body, which, in turn, enables the dreamer's mind and body to productively control sacred lucid dreams.

The main purpose for lucidity in Tenzin Rinpoche's sacred dream yoga is to overcome the mind's limitations in the lucid dream state and obtain what he refers to as flexibility of the mind. This achievement is important because a flexible mind can overcome rigidities of the psyche such as grasping and aversion, which trap the consciousness in a negative cycle of thought and keep it from being able to experience Ultimate Reality. Tenzin Rinpoche says there are eleven categories of experience in which the flexibility of the mind is limited. These can be overcome through sacred lucid dreaming, and he suggests ways to practice each.

First, he says the human mind is limited by the concept of size. Therefore, in lucid dreams you should practice making yourself larger or smaller. "Take a big problem and make it small," he recommends, or "take a small flower and make it as big as the sun." Second, in lucid dreams we should challenge quantity. If you dream of one Buddha, Tenzin Rinpoche maintains, increase the number to one hundred or one thousand. Make one thousand problems one. He says that while we are lucid, we should challenge the quality of dreams—especially those involving our feelings and emotions. Change the mood of a dream from anger to love, from sadness to joy. Tenzin Rinpoche maintains that once we can do this while dreaming, we will be able to do so in waking consciousness as well.

The speed with which things happen in dreams is capricious but manageable with lucidity. Tenzin Rinpoche suggests the dreamer try to slow down an experience until each moment is a whole world or to visit a hundred places in a minute. He also says you should enjoy the feeling of accomplishment in lucid dreams. Write a book, swim across an ocean, or finish a project that needs finishing. He relates a personal dream experience wherein his deceased mother visited him and asked him to build a stupa (a sanctuary structure to hold relics of a Buddha). He took the dream seriously but did not know how or where to begin building. In a subsequent dream he asked the dream guardians for help. They appeared in his dream and told him what he needed to know to complete the project, which he accomplished in his waking life.

A crucial concept of limitation that can be overcome in lucid dreaming is self-transformation. Tenzin Rinpoche says it is important to develop the ability to change your dream self into other forms in order to overcome habits that have become part of your personal identity. Of course, he suggests you transform yourself into a multitude of other forms—a dog, a lion, or a dragon. He also thinks it is important to practice transforming your state of mind within the dreamscape—from an angry person to a compassionate one, or from a grasping, jealous human into an open, clear buddha. Once the conceptual limits of transformation have been mastered in dream, the next step is to overcome the limit of emanation. Tenzin Rinpoche suggests using lucid dreaming to emanate oneself into two or more bodies to overcome your experience of the self as a single, separate ego.

The ability to journey at will is an aspect of Tibetan lucid dream yoga that seems to be universally exercised by lucid dreamers. Tenzin Rinpoche advises you to start with places you want to go—another country, another planet or star. But you should guide yourself consciously, because making the journey is more important than arriving there. Also test your limits of seeing in the lucid state. Try to see things you have never seen before—Guru Rinpoche, angels, Christ, cells dividing in your heart. Tenzin Rinpoche also discusses the importance of sacred dream presence encounters. When you encounter a deceased loved one, teacher, or guardian, he says you should ask for teaching. Finally, in lucid dreams you should transcend the normal conceptions of experience. Do something you have never done before—breathe water like a fish, walk through walls, become a cloud.[9]

Once you transcend these limitations in lucid dreams, Tenzin Rinpoche recommends you attempt to go beyond the limits of these categories to dissolve the boundaries that keep the mind from freely experiencing Ultimate Reality. "If you dream of a threatening fire, transform yourself into a flame; of a flood, transform yourself into water. If a demon chases you, transform yourself into a bigger demon." He goes on to assert that during lucid dreaming, you can and should stop at nothing to free the mind of its conventional limitations: "Become a mountain, a leopard, a redwood tree. Become a star, or an entire forest. Transform yourself from a man into a woman, and then into a hundred women. Or transform yourself from a woman into a goddess." He concludes:

> Lucidity brings more light to the conceptual mind, and exercising flexibility loosens the knots of conditioning that constrict it. As we are conditioned by the apparently solid entities we encounter, they should be transformed in our experience, made luminous and transparent. As we are conditioned by the apparent solidity of thoughts, they should be dissolved in the limitless freedom of the mind.[10]

Tenzin Rinpoche's sacred lucid dream advice can be somewhat startling for a variety of reasons to those with a Western mind-set. His approach to controlling the contents of the dream is quite aggressive, and he assumes a highly advanced proficiency of lucid dream technique. (Curiously, he also suggests you should dream yourself into the being of a buddha or a deity.) Seeing how much spiritual freedom, hope, and confidence Tenzin Rinpoche experiences in the art of sacred lucid dreaming is truly awe-inspiring, however. Whether we share the same methods and goals, we can learn much from the Tibetan Bön teachings.

The potential of human lucid dreaming ability that the Tibetan method acknowledges is so exhilarating that for some of us, it may seem a little intimidating. Marvelous heights and depths of sacred lucid dreaming can be reached, however, without the development of skills such as projecting the dream body into hundreds of other beings or becoming a mountain, forest, or goddess. We must remember that, in this tradition, lucidity is a tool for freeing the mind from restrictions for the sake of exiting from the cycle of rebirth. Therefore, the art of sacred dreaming is a preparatory skill, and the focus is not so much on the sacred experience of the dream itself. Although in the lucid dreams of visitation in which Tenzin Rinpoche honored the wishes of his mother, he suggested the dreamer ask for teaching upon encountering a teacher in the dream, he generally does not emphasize interaction between the lucid dreamer and the contents of the sacred dream itself. The reasons for this are clear, given the purpose of lucid dreaming and the religious goal it is used for.

Within my own cultural tradition and personal spiritual quest, however, my interest in sacred dreaming is centered on the spiritual quality of the dream experience. Therefore, for me and many of the sacred dreamers I have had the privilege to work with, lucidity is not only an effective tool for freeing the mind to reach Ultimate Reality, but an important means of interplay and communication with sacred dream events and figures.

Instead of simply watching the narrative of a sacred dream, as we often do in nonlucid dreaming, we can consciously enter the events of the mystical lucid dream to gain a clearer understanding of the sacred dream message or even to affect events. In the lucid state you can ask a sacred dream presence or visitor who he or she is and why he or she has come. In essence, you can perform the "Who are you?" sacred dream practice described in the previous chapter with the dream presence itself, within the dream. The power to consciously use your voice within these dreams can be life-changing. Conversations with sacred visitors are usually short, sweet, and simple, but profound.

With lucidity a dreamer can move toward, into, and through a spiritual beacon of light to fully experience the essence of its brilliance or the reality that lies beyond it. Fariba Bogzaran believes the phenomenon of light in lucid dreams serves as a hyperspace conduit for transition from "the familiar dreamscape to unfamiliar spaces in the mind." Bogzaran goes on to explain that for many sacred dreamers, the experience of inner light is one of joy, bliss, and oneness with the spirit world. "Depending on the level of the practitioner," Bogzaran says, "light consciousness opens to different levels of teaching. The seed of wisdom and many great teachings lie within the dimensions of inner light."[11]

Because, as we have seen, dream psychologist Tracey L. Kahan has scientifically proven that during the lucid dreaming of REM sleep the mind is capable of metacognitive skills, including self-reflection, intentionality, and self-regulation, lucid dreaming allows us not only to interact with mystical dream figures, light, events, and symbols, but to analyze and enhance the spiritual character of the dream itself, within the sequence of the dream. This capacity has tremendous ramifications for dreams that are highly charged with emotional or metaphorical value. If a mystical dreamer can reflectively question what aspect of her life is ending during a dream in which she is dying, not only will her questioning significantly alter the macabre mood of the dream, but she will also likely awaken with a feeling of empowerment—the sense of leaving behind something she no longer needs and looking forward to the prospects that are dawning as a result.

With lucidity, the nuances of mystical dreams of prophecy and reassurance can be affirmed within the sacred dream. In the same way, the confusion that often accompanies sacred dreams can be overcome, and, as we have seen, mystical nightmares can be transformed into wonderful dreams. Because the dream is largely driven by symbols and metaphors relevant to the dreamer's experience and emotional concerns, the ability to reason with intention and reflection during the lucid dream state allows the dreamer to analyze the symbolic content of the dream while it is going on. In turn, this enables the dreamer to take full advantage of the content and meaning of sacred dreams.

For example, while I was incubating sacred dreams with my sacred feather dreamsign, I concentrated on the image of the feather as I had consciously remembered it falling at my feet. After a few nights of setting this presleep sacred dream intention, I did dream of a fluffy white feather, falling, falling, falling in slow drifts in front of a backdrop of tall pine trees. I became lucid while watching the feather fall, and I immediately realized the sacred dream I had been cultivating had come to me. This thought occurred to me during the dream: though I had pictured the dove's feather lying still at my feet while incubating the dream, in all the stories I had drawn upon when I decided to work with this dream symbol, the way the feather had fallen into each narrative experience had been an important factor that I had not considered before.

I was also able to reason within the dream that this feather looked more like the one that a participant had encountered on the way to the seminar meeting and placed on the altar than the dove feather that I had used as my dreamsign. Other curiosities that I considered in the lucid state included that fact that though the feather that had fallen to my feet did so in front of the oak trees in my yard, this feather fell in front of lofty pines—a detail that was not included in any of the other feather stories that had been related to me.

I sensed within the dream that the feather knew something I did not and had a sacred message to impart. In this sense, I recognized that the feather represented a sacred presence for me in this dream, so I asked it, "Who are you?" At my question it twisted slightly upward as it continued to fall and caught a shaft of soft sunlight that subsided as quickly as it had appeared. "Why are you falling?" I asked. At this the feather gently landed on a bank of pure white, glistening snow and seemed to dissolve—white into white. As I woke up, I realized I was cold.

I was able to discern the message of the feathers upon later analysis of this dream, which I will explain in detail in chapter 6 on discerning the deep meaning of sacred dreams. But the central elements of this experience will help us understand the benefits of perfecting the art of sacred lucid dreaming. First, I knew I was dreaming, and therefore I was able to reason that this was the dream I had been incubating with my dream symbol. Second, I was able to reflect on how the feather in the dream compared and contrasted not only with the image of it I had been working with as I cultivated the dream, but also with the stories about the feathers that had appeared in the other instances that led me to use the feather as a dream symbol. Third, on the basis of that reflection, I was able to interact with the feather and affect the events of the dream by asking it who it was and why it was falling. As a result, I was given the extra symbols and clues I needed to derive the message of the sacred dream and the extraordinary means of spiritual fulfillment and personal growth it eventually blessed me with.

UNDERSTANDING AND MANEUVERING THE SACRED LUCID DREAM BODY

Because sacred lucid dreaming involves the active participation of the dreamer, a few words must be said about the nature of the body with which the dreamer interacts in the dream world. Many explanations have been offered in attempts to define what the dream body (or ethereal or astral body, as it has also been called) consists of. LaBerge's scientific opinion is that there is no such thing as a separate dream or astral body in the physical sense, but that whatever embodiment we perceive to have in dreams is the brain's memory of being connected to the physical body of waking consciousness.[12]

Tenzin Rinpoche discusses the *prana* energy centers of the body, which consist of root channels and psychic chakra centers, and the means of centering this energy with breath control before entering sleep and dream, but he does not discuss the nature of the dream body. According to *The Bliss of Inner Fire: Heart Practice of the Six Yogas of Naropa,* which explores dream yoga, however, a distinction is made between the gross (or physical) body of blood, bones, and sense organs, and the subtle body or *vajra* body of meditation and dreams. Of the energy channels and chakra centers involved in subtle body activity, the heart and throat energy centers control the energy of dreams. The Yogas of Naropa also distinguish between the subtle body and the "very subtle body" that manifests at the time of death.[13]

All I can say with certainty about this is that, from my own experience, when I arise and move about the world in lucid dreams, I am usually aware that I have left my physical body sleeping in my bed. At the same time, I am aware of the spiritual extensions of my dream body in such a manner that I sense it to be more than just a sensational mental memory of my physical body. I equate my dream body with my ensouled spiritual self. It is in this body or nature that I believe I will live on after the death of my physical body.

Lucid dreamers throughout history have reported experiences of the separation of the spiritual, astral, or ethereal self from the physical body during sleep. These have commonly become known as out-of-body experiences (OBEs). The Egyptians viewed the OBE as a soul-like essence that humans experience not only during sleep but also after death.

They called it *ba* and portrayed it in their hieroglyphs as a bird with a human head. Plato expressed his belief that the human soul could leave the body and travel, and this experience was recorded by many Christian saints and mystics.[14]

In the twentieth century, a variety of theosophical-style schools taught methods of astral or soul travel during lucid dream states. They recorded accounts about not only the dream body's adventures in heaven, hell, and other people's dreams, but also the ways the astral or soul body left the physical sleeping body. In many cases, it seemed to have gently risen. Other lucid dream travelers, however, experienced a buzzing and vibrating sensation that pulsated throughout the physical body at the separation. Because of this sensation, some lucid dreamers liken dreaming OBEs to the spiritual kundalini form of sexual energy, and in some traditions it has been regarded as a subtle form of spiritual eroticism. Sleep scientists have learned that these vibrations or the sensation of electrical currents running through the body can occur while the consciousness transitions from deeper stages of sleep into REM sleep. This would explain why they often seem to happen at the onset or in the midst of lucid dreaming when the dream body is distinguishing itself from the physical body.

Though I have drawn on LaBerge's lucid dream techniques, I believe lucid dreaming can be a foundational sacred experience and should be valued as such. Like the Tibetan Bön masters, I believe that lucid dreaming can be considered a human capability similar to what you encounter when passing from this life and into the next. I disagree, however, with those who hold that lucid dreaming is only a tool for teaching the mind to transcend the normal limits of consciousness in preparation for afterlife—whether it be reincarnation, liberation from the cycle of rebirth, or ascension into heaven. I am convinced that, when regarded and practiced as a high form of sacred art, every lucid dream can be a meaningful experience of noetic spiritual knowledge, growth, and fulfillment.

I have integrated elements of LaBerge's lucid dream techniques as well as some of the ritual techniques of the Tibetan Buddhist dream and sleep yogas in formulating my own method of guiding the mind toward sacred lucid dream activation and navigating the dream body through it. The following practice has worked well in facilitating my own lucid dream experience and has proven to be successful for sacred dreamers I have worked with.

Lucid Dreaming as a Sacred Art

1. Condition your mind for sacred lucid dreaming.

Throughout the day of waking consciousness, stop at intervals, look around, and deliberately relate to what you see and feel, while saying to yourself, "This is a dream. This is a wonderful, beautiful, sacred dream." Make sure you do this at least five times a day, but do it more often if you can. Say it while you do things you regularly observe as sacred—while praying, attending a church service, walking in the woods, watching a beautiful sunset. But also repeat this exercise while doing things you normally experience as mundane—washing dishes, filing papers, driving children to soccer practice. You may be struck by the realization that every aspect of your life is infused with spiritual energy.

As soon as you feel yourself being drawn into the sacred character of the moment in which you make your sacred dream acknowledgment, allow yourself to think or move through the mystical dreamscape you are experiencing. If this were a sleeping dream, what might happen next? How would you feel? What might you encounter as a sacred presence, and how might you interact with it? Naturally, you would not throw yourself off a

SKYLIGHT PATHS PUBLISHING
SUNSET FARM OFFICES RTE 4
PO BOX 237
WOODSTOCK VT   05091-0237

WIN A
$100
GIFT
CERTIFICATE!

Fill in this card and
mail it to us—
or fill it in online at

**skylightpaths.com/
feedback.html**

—to be eligible for a
$100 gift certificate for
SkyLight Paths books.

Fill in this card and return it to us to be eligible for our
quarterly drawing for a $100 gift certificate for SkyLight Paths books.

We hope that you will enjoy this book and find it useful in enriching your life.

Book title: _____

Your comments: _____

How you learned of this book: _____

If purchased: Bookseller _____ City _____ State _____

Please send me a free SkyLight Paths Publishing catalog. I am interested in: (check all that apply)

1. ❑ Spirituality
2. ❑ Mysticism/Kabbalah
3. ❑ Philosophy/Theology

4. ❑ Spiritual Texts
5. ❑ Religious Traditions (Which ones?) _____
6. ❑ Children's Books

7. ❑ Prayer/Worship
8. ❑ Meditation
9. ❑ Interfaith Resources

Name (PRINT) _____

Street _____

City _____ State _____ Zip _____

E-MAIL (FOR SPECIAL OFFERS ONLY) _____

Please send a SkyLight Paths Publishing catalog to my friend:

Name (PRINT) _____

Street _____

City _____ State _____ Zip _____

SKYLIGHT PATHS® Publishing Tel: (802) 457-4000 • Fax: (802) 457-4004

Available at better booksellers. Visit us online at www.skylightpaths.com

building expecting to be able to fly, as you might be able to in your dream body, but allow yourself the luxury of experiencing waking life reality in the manner of a lucid dream to the fullest extent that you can.

For several reasons, I find the method of reminding myself on a regular basis that "this is a dream, a wonderful, beautiful, sacred dream" is more conducive to cultivating spiritual lucid dreams than LaBerge and Rheingold's method of asking yourself whether you are dreaming. First, my method honors the continuum of the sacred character of the personal psyche between states of consciousness as well as the experience of life as a sacred process of spiritual understanding, growth, and renewal. Second, gently reminding ourselves of the sacred dreamlike quality of life throughout the day gives us occasion to periodically leave the pressures and cares of our regular business and truly appreciate the beautiful, sacred character of our existence in this remarkable world. In this respect, reminding ourselves that life is a wonderful, beautiful, sacred dream gives us space to live within the sacred fullness of the moment, and as Tenzin Rinpoche maintains, it helps us to live our waking lives with more "lucidity."

A third reason I personally prefer repeatedly making myself aware of the dream quality of this wonderful and beautiful life is not only that it continually helps to refocus my attitude about life in a positive way, but that it also helps to cultivate a sleep-dreaming consciousness more prone to wander into wondrous and positive mystical dreamscapes than into those that might result in nightmarish scenes or sensations.

2. Perform presleep sacred dream rituals.

At this time you are probably still experimenting with or settling into your own presleep dream ritual sequence, which should include dietary and cleansing purification, light or fire, and some form of physical body involvement, whether it be movement or voice. Perform whatever method is most conducive to sacred dreaming for you, but direct your psyche toward sacred lucid dreaming by reminding yourself throughout your ritual, "This is a dream, a wonderful, beautiful sacred dream," and experience the fullness of your ritual as such.

3. Practice presleep sacred lucid dream meditation and intention.

You do not need to tell yourself you are dreaming after you lie down. If you have done this several times throughout the day, the instruction should be programmed into your consciousness well enough that it will likely repeat itself automatically during a REM sleeping cycle. At this point, free your mind of everything but pre-sleep meditative breathing and your lucid dream intentions.

As in the previous sacred dream practices, lie in a comfortable position and straighten your spine. To integrate more of the Tibetan Bön method of presleep meditative breath ritual, men can lie on their right side and women on their left. The reason for this position is that it puts restrictive pressure on the white energy channel, where it is believed negative emotions circulate, and opens the red energy channel, where positive emotional energy flows. Take a deep, comfortable breath, and feel it as soft, bright light traveling the length of your spine. Hold the breath momentarily, feeling its energy radiate in the area between your throat and heart. Exhale slowly. Repeat breathing in this manner until you are completely relaxed and the breathing becomes natural enough to continue without mental effort.

As you continue to breathe, declare emphatically, "Tonight when I dream, I will become lucid." If you have been focusing on a sacred dream symbol that has been working for you or have come to recognize a recurring dream pattern, integrate this into your declaration. For example, I might have said, "Tonight when I see a feather falling, I will know I am dreaming and will become lucid." Adding a dreamsign affords two cognitive tools with which to help your sleeping mind recognize it is dreaming and achieve a state of lucidity. When you see the sign in your dream, you will probably automatically say to yourself, "This is a dream, a wonderful, beautiful, sacred dream." You may also add to your presleep avowal a sacred lucid dream request or intention, such as, "Tonight when I realize I am in the company of a deceased loved one, I will know I am dreaming, and I will ask him what heaven is like."

The key is to pattern your declaration on whatever you think is most likely to happen in the dream state that you might recognize from your prior dreaming experience and to use this as a conscious guide to prompt lucidity and a meaningful sacred dream experience. Above all, as least once make the declaration emphatically and audibly to the cosmos and your psyche, and then repeat it in your mind in rhythm with your meditative breathing until you fall asleep. If you wake up without memory of having had a sacred lucid dream, repeat the process. Remember, most people have longer periods of REM sleep in the early morning hours, after they have already passed through a couple of sleep cycles. You might need to practice this sequence a few nights before you experience a sacred lucid dream; however, with the dreaming process, persistence will almost always be eventually rewarded.

4. Navigate your dream psyche and body to and through the sacred aspects of your lucid dream.

If you have had experience with lucid dreams, you may already have developed a means of navigating yourself consciously and physically through them. If you have not, when you first become aware that you are asleep and dreaming, affirm to yourself that you are dreaming and take a moment to appreciate the freedom and fluidity of your dream body. If you cannot seem to raise your dream body from the bed, relax and watch the dream with mild curiosity. You will probably drift back into a short interval of dreamless sleep and revert quickly to a lucid dream in which you are already up and ready for action. Test some of your regular limitations—for example, by trying to fly or change your physical size or shape—in the manner suggested by LaBerge and Tenzin Rinpoche's Tibetan lucid dream yogas. Then reaffirm the fact that you are experiencing a wonderful, beautiful, sacred dream, and start to notice or sense what is sacred at work within the dream.

If you see or sense a sacred presence, interact with it in the way that seems most appropriate. A better way to think about this step might be to concentrate on trying to articulate your relationship with that presence and then to act accordingly. For example, you might feel compelled to move near the presence of a deceased close loved one and to talk with compassion and relative freedom; however, you may well approach the presence of a divinity with a little more awe and reverence. In many cases, you may find yourself in the company of someone or something you sense has spiritual significance but not be sure why it is significant, in which case you might be prudent not to make a move one way or another but just to wait and see what happens. If talking with the presence feels right, ask the presence whatever questions seem appropriate, such as "Who are you?" "Why have you come into my dream?" "Do you have a message for me?" "Is there something you want me to do for you?" or "How should I deal with such-and-such problem?"

I have found that most people who have sacred dreams of pure or intense light usually feel compelled to move toward it and, if possible, enter it. In some cases the light moves toward them or is present within their dream bodies from the onset of lucidity. In other cases, however, a divine light seems unapproachable or seems to purposely deflect the movement of the dreamer.

The narrative and emotional content of all dreams, especially those of a spiritual nature, is personal, so I can give you no better advice on how to move through sacred lucid dreams than to try to identify what is mystical within the dreamscape and then to follow your own instincts. In most cases, however, trying to respectfully engage the dream presence in dialogue will usually help to explain the significant message of the dream within the dream itself or will give valuable clues with which you can work later.

Again, persistence is the foundational attribute of sacred dreaming. The more you practice these sacred lucid dream techniques, the more you will experience sacred lucid dreaming, and the better you will become at navigating yourself through them. And ultimately, the sacred art of dreaming will enrich your life with spiritual wisdom and growth on an entirely new level.

Part Three

Interpreting Dreams
as a Sacred Art

CHAPTER FIVE

SACRED DREAM RECALL

The art of working with sacred dreams depends upon on the dreamer's ability to recognize the symbols and symbolic patterns that make up his own sacred psychic reality. In other words, as we have seen, what we experience as sacred is encoded in each individual's consciousness with a particular set of associations that tend to manifest themselves metaphorically in dreams and more subtly in waking life. We have also discussed the importance of establishing conscious continuity between sacred sleeping dreams and waking sacred consciousness, and we have practiced techniques for maintaining the relationship between the two while passing from wakefulness into sleep and eventually into the sacred dreamscape. In this section, we will complete the cycle. We'll explore several methods of carrying the sacred dream consciousness back into waking consciousness in order to work with the dream consciousness as part of an organic sacred psychic experience. This can spiral us into new realms of spiritual awareness and growth. Before we can attempt to do this, however, we must be able to remember what we dreamt, so we can later identify its sacred character and intent.

When people learn that I conduct seminars on sacred dreaming, they often feel compelled to share a little of their personal dream history with me. I am amazed how many of them starkly state that they do not dream at all. When I tell them that sleep and dream psychologists have proven beyond a doubt that everyone dreams, and our mental, emotional, and physical health depends on dreaming at regular intervals during sleep, many of them will still flatly assert that they do not. Even more people I talk with are aware that they dream regularly but rarely remember what they dreamt and do not seem to be particularly interested in doing so. Nevertheless, most of these dreamers of phantom dreams will be able to recall one or two dreams that they have had—usually in youth or the distant past, when they were undergoing some traumatic or life-changing experience.

The reason many of us who live in the Western world often have no dream recollection at all or are able to remember only one or two sporadic significant dreams is probably that in our culture we do not place a great deal of emphasis on our personal dream lives. I find this curious, given that so many contemporary movies and television shows deal with dream sequences or dream phenomena. Upon further examination of dream scenarios presented in modern media shows, however, we see that they typically support popular themes that are often based on violence and sex, and have relatively little to do with the true nature of human dreaming, much less sacred dreaming. In effect, the way dreams have been commoditized only serves to further alienate the dreamer from the true and sacred nature of her dream life.

Psychologists have provided a number of scientific explanations for why we remember some dreams and not others. One observation is that we are more prone to remember dreams when we wake up soon after them and less likely to remember them the longer we sleep after the dream sequence ends. Note that sleep and dream researchers have discovered that most

adults naturally wake up at least momentarily at the completion of each sleep cycle, usually after a stretch of REM sleep,
during which we are most likely to dream. Unfortunately, we
tend to fall back asleep so quickly that we rarely recognize we
woke up at all, much less that we were just dreaming.

Most people, including those who are not conscious of their
regular dreams, will remember at least one significant dream.
According to Jung, the occasional significant, life-changing,
emotionally charged dream that the dreamer usually remem-
bers for the rest of her life may "prove to be the richest jewel
in the treasure-house of psychic experience."[1] Given that
Bulkeley's study on sacred dreaming revealed that most people
described their most memorable dream as a sacred or mystical dream, these big dreams are important to take into account
when cultivating the art of working with sacred dreams. They
cannot tell the whole story about how the Sacred works through
our dreaming consciousness and integrates with our waking
consciousness to speak to each of us, however. For this, we need
to be able to access the sacred dreams we routinely experience
but often fail to remember.

Fortunately, some effective techniques for improving sacred
dream recall have been identified. The first step is simply to be
more aware of your sacred dream potential and activity. Just as
intensified interest in dreaming and dream work increases the
ability to incubate and navigate through dreams, it also helps
to improve our ability to remember them upon waking. Other
techniques for enhancing sacred dream recall include heighten-
ing your awareness of waking intervals between sleep cycles,
sacred dream rehearsal, and keeping a dream journal.

WAKING BETWEEN SLEEP CYCLES

In the same manner that you can condition your sleeping consciousness to enter a sacred dream and navigate through it with

lucidity, you can also condition it to be more mindful of your natural sleep cycle. Chances are you are already in the habit of waking around a certain time every night or early morning, which would indicate the completion of one cycle. Add and subtract ninety-minute intervals from this time, and you will have a pretty good idea of how your natural sleep pattern is punctuated. If you tell yourself that you will wake up long enough to remember what you were dreaming at these times, you will be more apt to do so.

THE ART OF DREAM REHEARSAL

Just as focusing on a dream symbol helps build a bridge of consciousness between wakefulness and dream sleep, the art of dream rehearsal is the most effective way to span the conscious psychic rift that usually occurs between dreamful sleep and waking. Dream rehearsal should be practiced as soon after waking as possible. Acting quickly is essential for this technique, because huge parts of the dream sequence and major symbolic dream clues can dissolve from memory within seconds as the brain habitually reorients itself to waking consciousness. Dream rehearsal consists of rethinking the self through whatever can be remembered of the dream. The rehearsal is different from simply trying to remember the action of the dream. By reintegrating the waking consciousness with the sleeping-dream consciousness, you will more likely relive the dream from the perspective of the dream body and its psychic workings.

Rehearsing the dream as it happened in sleeping consciousness is crucial because, for those of us who were not raised in a culture that values the benefits of our dream lives, dream experience and reasoning happen on a level of psychic activity different from waking life experience and reasoning. In his treatise "The Structure of the Psyche," Jung distinguishes between what he calls directed and undirected thought.[2]

Thought that is directed by language is intrinsically different from undirected or dreamlike thought, because the thought processes we use during dreams are more similar to the way people thought before the emergence of language systems—in clusters of images. These dream image clusters are laden with patterns of symbols and metaphors that speak to us on a level deeper than the symbol system of language. Therefore, initially reliving the dream scenario rather than redescribing it in mental or vocal words is important. It helps to preserve the dream's natural integrity and symbolic impact before it is transcribed into the symbol system of language in the following step, dream journaling.

Dream-thought symbols are often related to the language symbol systems we are educated with, but they speak to us in dreams in a different manner. For example, the common dream of falling often reflects the connotations of "falling" in language. In English we use phrases like "falling from grace," "falling out of favor," and "falling in love." Falling dreams can signify any of these realities or concerns, as well as many other idioms about falling. Within the falling experience of the dream, however, an infinite number of other symbolic nuances—beyond the realm of language—will occur. These indicate not only which of these scenarios is actually being played out in the depths of the consciousness, but how and why.

Most dream interpretation guides urge the dreamer to record the dream as soon after waking as possible. Nonetheless, I have found that, especially when working with sacred dream content, rehearsing the dream first is essential. It can help the dreamer remember not only the narrative of the dream, but how it shifts from one cluster of images to another, as well as a host of symbolic details like colors, numbers, shapes, environments, movements, and so on. Rehearsing the dream reinforces the impact of any information gleaned through sacred lucid dream navigation and revitalizes the relationship sensed between the dreamer and the sacred dream presence.

Anthropologist and dream analyst Michele Stephen argues that the mind contains two separate registers of memory—one that "organizes information in terms of verbal categories and semantic understandings" and another one that "records and organizes all information according to its emotional significance."[3] Because we dream with the emotionally coded consciousness, our memory of the dream is charged with our feelings about what we encounter in dreams. These often get lost when the dream is committed to the written word before it is adequately relived through the dream memory consciousness. In short, dream rehearsal keeps the emotional atmosphere of the dream alive. And because our emotional connection with what we hold sacred in our dreaming and waking consciousness is of utmost importance, it is an integral step in the art of working with sacred dreams.

THE ART OF KEEPING A SACRED DREAM JOURNAL

As soon after the dream feels it is as well rehearsed as possible, the dreamer should record it, being especially attentive to the unique character of the dream thought symbolism and expressing the nuances in language. I prefer to record my dreams in a personal dream journal, with the intent that it will never be seen by anyone else. The reason for this is not so much to preserve privacy about the actual dream content, though this is important, but to free me from the conventional bounds of language and help me to record the dream in a way that reflects its natural character.

Keeping a sacred dream journal is perhaps the most important step in the art of working with sacred dreams. Through the mental process of transposing the contents of a sleeping dream to waking life language, all sorts of psychic realities can become evident. The dream journal allows us to use our nightly dreams to connect the dots between the big mystical dreams, which in turn enables us to trace the deep-conscious road map that has been trying to lead us to the heights and depths of our spiritual awareness and potential.

How you choose to construct your dream journal is a matter of personal taste, and for those who are anxious to explore their sacred dream life as an aesthetic form of art, creating a journal can be an integral and satisfying part of the whole process of dreaming as a sacred art. As you start or develop your own journal, keep in mind the following principles.

1. Whether you prefer to handwrite your dreams or use a computer or other electronic device, make sure you keep whatever you need within easy reach of where you sleep and dream. Many dreams you will rehearse and want to record may occur before your final sleep cycle of the night when you are apt to fall back asleep at any moment. So having to take even one step out of bed to access your writing instruments might be enough to inhibit you from recording a significant amount of dream content.

2. A lamp with a three-way bulb is also a good thing to have within arm's reach. Being able to gradually adjust the light helps ease the assault of light on undilated pupils in the middle of the night. Little things like this can make a difference in whether you choose to write down your dream while you are probably still feeling groggy.

3. Keep all your dream journal entries together and in sequential order. If you record them on a computer, keep them in a well-organized file. After years of keeping a dream journal, I have come to prefer using

a loose-leaf notebook, because it allows me to add pages or artwork that I generate in later dream interpretation or healing work. I like to use a notebook with a transparent shield on the front, so I can design and insert my own cover, and I insert every page in a plastic sleeve. I admit this step is time-consuming, but as you work with your sacred dream journal, it becomes such a valuable and tangible expression of your spiritual self that it quickly turns into a labor of love and endless gratification.

4. If you use a hard-copy format for your dream journal, record your dreams on the left-hand page of a two-page layout. This leaves space on the right-hand page for later dream interpretation work, which will be discussed in the next chapter. Of course, if you record your dream journal with a computer word processor, later work can be easily inserted.

5. If you have not already done so, record in your journal any significant or "big" mystical dreams you have had in the past. Not only will this form a good foundation for your subsequent sacred dream journal entries, but Aizenstat says this is the most effective way of stimulating your conscious for better future dream recall.[4]

Sacred Dream Recall

1. Set a sacred dream recall intention.

Before you go to sleep, tell yourself firmly that whenever you awaken during the night or in the morning, you will remember what you were dreaming. This practice can easily be integrated into whatever dream intentions you are already working with. For example, you might say, "Tonight when I dream, I will know that I am dreaming, and I will be open to the presence of the Divine. When I awake, I will remember my dream."

2. Ask yourself what you were just dreaming.

As soon as you are aware that you have awakened, ask yourself, "What was I just dreaming?" This is more effective than asking yourself whether you were dreaming, because unless you are awakened by an alarm or some other external stimulus, you are most likely to wake up after the REM dreaming portion of your natural sleep cycle, in which case you were probably dreaming. Asking yourself whether you were dreaming not only wastes precious dream consciousness recall time, but also partially closes off your waking consciousness to the possibility that you were dreaming. This interruption can thwart the rehearsal process. With practice, you can train yourself to ask yourself what you were dreaming before you open your eyes. Ideally, you will develop the ability to do your entire dream rehearsal in this manner— before you open your eyes at all—while your conscious is still as much in the dream memory mode as possible.

Do not be concerned if you are able to remember only a small slice of a dream while being aware that there was much more to it. This experience is fairly common. If this is the case, try to remember what preceded whatever you can remember. Often the previous scenarios will pop into your mind. If it does not, simply work with what you do remember. It is probably the part of the dream that contains the core of the message the dream was trying to relate. If you have no dream recall at all, repeat your dream recall intention before you go back to sleep. Again, because most of us experience longer periods of REM sleep as our sleep cycles progress, you will likely have longer, more vivid, and more memorable dreams in later sleep cycles, which for those who sleep at night will be in the morning. This is probably as good an excuse for sleeping late as you will ever get, so enjoy!

3. Rehearse your dream.

Using all your senses, immediately review whatever you can remember about your dream. Be conscious of being back in the
dreamscape, in your dream body, and engaging in the dream
sequence from the same perspective with which your sleeping
conscious dreamt it. Take note of every detail—what you see,
what you hear, how things smell, how something tastes, what you
touch or what touches you, and how you feel in general. This
information is important, because a sacred presence or spiritual
communication in dreams is often largely felt or sensed.

Ideally, you are able to rise at this moment and write in your
journal about the dream, but if you feel as though you will drift
back to sleep, keep rehearsing the dream until you do. The more
you rehearse it, the better your chances of remembering it when
you finally get up and commit it to writing.

4. Record your dream.

Keeping a thoughtful dream journal is not only a fundamental
part of dream recall, but the foundation of sacred dream interpretation. Even if you are interested only in working with your mystical or spiritual dreams, do not make the mistake of neglecting to
record dreams that did not seem to exhibit any sacred content
during the rehearsal. You will be amazed how many times during
interpretation a sacred dream intention you have been cultivating
will suddenly manifest itself where you least expected it. Often
these dreams—the quiet ones that did not initially seem important—will suddenly supply the missing metaphorical link that can
illuminate the deeper spiritual meaning of a string of more obviously sacred dreams.

I recommend keeping a journal of your dreams in the form
of what cultural anthropologist Clifford Geertz calls a "thick description."[5] In his book *The Interpretation of Cultures*, Geertz was
interested in analyzing the codes or symbols that underlie cultural religious ritual. Because religious ritual is the enactment of

a religious story or myth, and mythology is the cultural form of undirected or dream thought, I have found this approach to be very successful for dream journaling and interpretation.

The aim is to keep a journal of the dream content while trying to unpack all the details from the very thick of the dream experience. In other words, place yourself mentally and emotionally back into the dream rehearsal, and make note of every detail, from every level of consciousness, that you possibly can. Feel free to include drawings or colored images. I like to keep soft colored pencils and pastels handy. Not only do they enable me to add to my journal brilliant colors close to those that I tend to dream in, but the pastels can be smeared into the amorphous images or feelings about images I tend to encounter in dreams. If you choose to use pastels, keep paper towels handy as well, because pastels are usually oil based and will stain textiles. Even if something you recall from the dream seems insignificant at the time, record it in whatever manner seems most accurate, with full attention to every detail.

Sometimes when dream recall escapes us upon awakening, we will get flashes of a dream at odd intervals later in the day—probably because we are doing or sensing something at that point in waking life that we associate on some level with the contents of the dream we had the night before. If this happens, stop what you are doing, if possible, and rehearse with full attention whatever glimpse of the dream image you experienced. Often more of the dream will manifest itself, but whether or not it does, be sure to write in your journal whatever you do remember as soon as you can, along with details about what you were doing when the dream twinkled in your waking psyche. Even if you just have a feeling about something, it might end up speaking volumes in further dream analysis.

As Geertz notes, this sort of data collection contains a "multiplicity of complex conceptual structures, many of them superimposed upon or knotted into one another." He adds that they are often "strange, irregular, and inexplicit."[6] This is especially true of dreams, and it is why LaBerge and Rheingold relied on examining the irregularities they encountered as a means of inducing the lucid state while dreaming. The more curious or out of place something seems, the more likely it is to contain dream-encoded symbolic significance. Therefore, if you really want to do deep sacred dream work, do not neglect to write down the weird stuff that you just cannot believe came out of your own consciousness—no matter how bizarre or even embarrassing it might seem. The point is that it might not have come entirely out of your own consciousness and, once interpreted, might serve as a mystical portal to worlds of spiritual meaning and self-awareness.

CHAPTER SIX

THE ART OF
DISCERNING THE
DEEP MEANING OF
SACRED DREAMS

Because I was raised with a Western Christian worldview, I have learned to regard time and all endeavors that take place within time as linear. In other words, everything has a beginning, several points of interest along the way, and an eventual end. When I started working with my sacred dreams, I tended to treat my dream work as a linear process that began with dream incubation, continued with navigation and interpretation, and ended with some sort of acknowledgment or expression of enrichment or healing.

After many years of studying the vast array of the world's religions and their historical philosophies, however, the doors to my conceptual understanding of sacred time were flung wide open when I learned that, in the Eastern consciousness, time is treated not as linear, but rather as more of a circling or even spiraling of awareness. How very different everything becomes from this perspective. How freeing every endeavor seems when there is no pressure to regard it as another task that must have recognizable beginning and ending points and milestones marking progress along the way. Integrating this view into my attitude about sacred dreaming has opened a new dimension of the art for me. Regarding it as an ever-spiraling process of incubation, navigation, interpretation, acknowledgment, and enrichment—the fruits of which can be fed right back into another round of incubation, navigation, and so on—allows the dreamer to live in an exhilarating continuum of spiritual awareness, depth, and growth.

The interpretation of the wisdom sacred dreams are trying to impart is the aspect of this high art that drives the whole process and keeps it spiraling in a meaningful direction. Therefore, discerning the deep meaning of the sacred dream is the heart of dreaming as a sacred art. I have crafted my own method for this step, following the same process I used for dream cultivation—examining noteworthy historical methods of sacred and psychological dream interpretation, extrapolating the ritual steps of these methods that appear to be universal, and reconstructing these common ritual dream interpretation techniques into a method that is meaningful and productive for the contemporary sacred dreamer.

HISTORICAL METHODS OF
SACRED DREAM INTERPRETATION

The art of sacred dream interpretation has a deeply rooted and multifaceted history. Evidence in Chinese bone inscriptions of its use as a means of divination dates as far back as 2000 BCE. From the fragments that remain, we can discern that the earliest kings of China, who were essentially warrior shamans, relied on auspicious spiritual dreams, in conjunction with observing how bones cracked when heated and in divining and prophesying the best time to wage war, among other royal endeavors. Bulkeley explains that the interpretation of dreams eventually became an officially sanctioned practice of the royal court. By the time of the Zhou dynasty (about 1100 BCE) a high position called *tai pu* was held by someone who was considered an expert on dream interpretation and other methods of divinization—usually a mystically gifted peasant woman.[1] In addition to oracular divination, other methods of historical Chinese dream interpretation included "comparing dream images to common symbols from waking life, linguistically analyzing them for puns and word play, and religiously associating them to classic texts and beloved teachers." By contrast, Taoist texts claim that "the ultimate interpretation is to let go of the grasping, entangling desire to know what any dream means."[2]

The sacred dreams recorded in texts from Mesopotamia, Egypt, and Greece are described as experiences in which a deity appears at the head of a sleeping person, usually a ruler, to deliver a prophetic message.[3] Such dreams were often interpreted for the king by a goddess or priestess. In addition to deciphering the sacred meaning of the message, interpreters analyzed dreams for their symbolic content and scrutinized literary puns in them. In these traditions it was believed that homonyms (words that sound alike but have different meanings) or words that have more than one meaning affected the meaning of the dream. For example, in the *Epic of Gilgamesh*, the hero dreams: "The stars of the heavens gathered to me and a meteorite from Anum fell on top [*tseri*] of me."[4] When the dream is interpreted by his mother, the goddess Ninsun, she associates the word used for the act of the meteor "landing on top" of Gilgamesh, *tseri*, with its homonym, which means "born of the steppeland." With this literary twist, she reads the dream to foretell the arrival of Enkidu, the "man of the steppeland," who did indeed "land on top of," or surprise, Gilgamesh with his appearance.[5] The ancient Egyptians were particularly interested in interpreting sacred symbolic dream wordplay. To dream of a harp, which can be transliterated from Egyptian hieroglyphs as *bnt,* could indicate that something evil (*bint*) was about to happen. A dream of a donkey (*az*) could be interpreted as an upcoming promotion (*saz*).[6]

The sacred dreams recorded in the Hebrew Scriptures are also interpreted through symbols and wordplay. The most noteworthy biblical dream interpreter was Joseph, who, while imprisoned, explained the sacred messages of Pharaoh's dreams and thus earned his freedom and a high position in Pharaoh's court. A close reading of Joseph's interpretations of the other inmates' dreams shows that they were largely based on literary puns. As in the Mesopotamian dreams, biblical dreams also tended to be understood as sacred messages intended for the king or ruler. As biblical studies professor Scott Noegel notes, they often served to "legitimate the political, national, or military concerns of the dreamer."[7]

In Islamic sacred texts it is reported that the Prophet (Muhammad) said, "A dream will take effect according to how it is interpreted."[8] From this perspective, the interpretation of the dream becomes more important than the dream itself. Classical Islamic literature says that good or righteous dreams come from God, while deceptive or impure dreams come from the Devil. In the fourteenth century, the Muslim philosopher Ibn Khaldun clarified this even further in explaining, "Clear dreams come from God. Allegorical dream visions, which call for interpretation, come from the angels. And 'confused dreams' come from Satan."[9] Ibn Khaldun asserted, "God intentionally created sleep as an opportunity for humans to 'lift the veil of the senses' and gain access to divine realities and higher forms of knowing."[10]

The examination of dream symbols is also an integral aspect of dream interpretation in this tradition, and ancient Muslim dream manuals provide a catalogue of symbolic dream categories, such as dreams of the Prophet, fish, flowers, and occupations.[11]

Other methods of dream interpretation include identifying correspondence between dream content and verses in the Qur'an, the Prophet's sayings, proverbs, and poetry; examining dream content for increase or decrease; considering the content's opposite meaning; and taking into consideration the conditions that affect the dreamer, such as the state of his health or the time of year.[12] As illustrated earlier in the case of Istikhara, Muslim dream incubation and interpretation has traditionally been used as a method of divination.

Western methods of dream interpretation have their roots in Greek and Roman philosophy. In Homer's *Odyssey,* the Land of Dreams was the last stop on the way to the land of the dead, indicating that dreams were considered otherworldly. In Hesiod's *Theogony,* the earliest Greek creation story, written about 800 BCE, the dream realm was one of the first creations after the gods and the earth arose. In Socrates's dialogue with Plato, he analyzed a dream he had in which a goddess-like figure in white brought him a symbolic omen of his death. Plato's dreaming was often troubled by what he regarded as animalistic spirits, and he warned against allowing them to influence your waking life. He did allow for the possibility, however, that one who is of "clear self-consciousness" could dream guided by pure reason, with "the divine soul liberated from the sleeping body and capable of gaining true insight and trans-temporal knowledge."[13] Aristotle was also suspicious of the use of dream interpretation as a means of psychological or sacred self-understanding. In two short treatises on the subject, he analyzed sleep and dream phenomena in terms of natural law and physics. He warned against the use of dreams as a means of divination and dismissed prophetic dreams as "mere coincidences in which people mistakenly perceive a connection between a dream and an external event."[14]

This negative attitude toward the interpretation and practical use of dreams in the Greco-Roman world influenced early

Christian doctrine. Jerome, a fourth-century monk and principal translator of the Latin Vulgate Bible, discouraged the use of dream interpretation. After a traumatic dream in which he was swept up to heaven and received a divine reprimand and physical punishment for studying "pagan" Greek philosophy, he associated dream interpretation with other forms of divination that had been labeled pagan and forbidden. Jerome set the standard for Christian skepticism about the value of dream interpretation. Some of the most influential later Christian theologians, such as Augustine and Thomas Aquinas, also cast a suspicious eye on the sacred character of human dreaming, because they believed it could not be rationally controlled.

In response to negative attitudes about dreams and the importance of their influence on everyday life, the professional diviner Artemidorus of Daldis wrote the *Oneirocritica*, or *Interpretation of Dreams,* in the second century CE in Asia Minor. The primary focus of this study was to classify common dreams and their typical meanings. Artemidorus recognized two types of dreams—those that deal with the present and those that foretell future events. He also distinguished between dreams that were direct in their content and those that were allegorical—that is, composed of indirect imagery, symbols, and metaphor. Within these latter dreams, he wrote, "The soul is conveying something obscurely by physical means."[15] As Bulkeley notes, Artemidorus obviously believed in the sacred character of dreams and the prophetic power of the human soul. He also underscored throughout the book his belief that the only true basis for interpreting a dream is personal experience. The *Oneirocritica* has become the foundational work on dream interpretation for the Western world.

As indicated in ancient Islamic dream guides, the belief that a paradoxical interpretation of dreams can be an effective method of figuring out what the deep consciousness is trying to convey to us is shared by other cultural religious traditions as well. This method is commonly used in indigenous African religions. Bulkeley says that, while from a modern perspective we might find absurd the claim that the contents of a dream indicate that we can expect the exact opposite to happen in waking life,

> paradoxical interpretations tap into a genuine truth about the dreaming mind, namely, the binary quality of certain images and themes. Few cognitive scientists would dispute that an oppositional logic governs many of the basic metaphysical categories used in waking thought and language.[16]

METHODS OF PSYCHOLOGICAL DREAM INTERPRETATION

Freud is often credited with establishing the basic principles for psychological study of dream interpretation, though much of his work on the subject was borrowed from his predecessors in the field, who were probably not fairly acknowledged. Nonetheless, in letters to his colleagues he asserted that "the secret of dreams" had been revealed to him.[17] He published *The Interpretation of Dreams* at the beginning of the twentieth century. In it, he advanced his theory that dreams are made up of information that has been generated from two distinct psychological levels, which he called manifest and latent content. The manifest content is the part of the dream that is easily remembered, which in his estimation is merely a disguised representation of latent content, unconscious activity underlying the dream. This latent content is made up of ungratified wishes and fantasies, which Freud believed were always due to a deep-rooted psychosexual need or desire. "Dreamwork," as Freud understood it, is the mind's business of transforming the latent content into manifest content.

Therefore, Freud's methods of dream interpretation involved trying to discern the latent content that prompted the manifest content of the dream narrative, which he also understood as coded in metaphor. Freud used his method of free association to help his patients interpret the meanings of their dream symbols. In effect, if a patient reported dreaming of a snake, he would have her randomly recite everything else that automatically came to her mind when she thought about a snake—words like slithery, scaly, sneaky, frightening, and so on. He would use these free associations to unravel the deeper meaning of the dream. Freud also relied on a technique he said "never failed," in which he asked the dreamer to repeat the same dream twice. He believed that subtle changes between one telling and the next revealed a "weak spot" in the dream's disguise that might expose the latent content for deeper analysis.[18]

Jung worked closely with Freud in the early part of his career as a depth psychologist. But the two went their separate ways when Jung expressed his disagreement with Freud's theory that the sexual libido was the driving force of all unconscious motivation. Jung was fascinated with dream interpretation and avidly worked with his own dreams, many of which he recorded and depicted visually in his autobiography, *Memories, Dreams, Reflections,* and in his more recently published *Red Book.* His belief that dreams can access the collective unconscious (mental remnants of humanity's ancient past imprinted in the unconscious) resulted from his interpretation of a series of dreams he experienced throughout his life in which he was continually descending to subterranean regions and digging up ancient bones. For him, this was symbolic of his vocation, which he decided was to help people discover the archaic remnants that drove their dreams and psychological concerns.

Jung's system of dream symbol analysis is sophisticated and aimed at discerning the archetypes—typical modes of perception—derived from the psyche's experience with the collective unconscious within the dream. He demonstrated this method in detail in his book *Psychology and Alchemy,* in which he analyzed four hundred dreams from over a thousand recorded by a young scientist. Jung noted the recurring symbol of the mandala (Sanskrit for "sacred circle") in a majority of the dreams. Eventually, he found strong similarities between many of the detailed accounts of the mandalas and other symbols in the scientist's dreams, and mandala motifs and symbols found in drawings of medieval alchemists—especially in works concerning the methods with which they attempted to transform base substances into gold, which for Jung symbolized immortality.

Though the young man had no prior knowledge of the alchemical process, Jung believed it had been imprinted in his unconscious as an archetypal symbolic pattern. Linking the underlying core value of the alchemists' work—obtaining immortality—to the symbolism of the mandala, which Jung believed was self-healing energy, he interpreted the series of dreams to be self-healing and revitalizing messages. These were aided through the young man's ability to access the archetypal energy of his collective consciousness.[19]

Jung also believed that humans have psychic archetypal senses of self that often manifest in dreams. I have personally found this aspect of his work to be important for interpreting the deep meaning of sacred dreams. The first time I read his theory about how we carry our deep selves in archetypal patterns in dreams, I immediately began to feel their presence in my own dreams. Once they are found, they profoundly speak the pith of the dream's meaning.

The persona archetype is like a mask and is worn in dreams in which the dreamer plays out aspects of her waking life relationships and social roles. The shadow archetype is a manifestation of the dreamer's dark side, which often represents repressed aspects of the dreamer's personality or concept of his other self. The shadow is often portrayed within the dream as an external human figure or as a sister or brother (strong archetypes of other self in mythology). I do not often think about the shadow within my dream, but after rehearsing and journaling, I sometimes realize I had the strong sense that something or someone was looking over my shoulder or standing behind me for all or part of the dream. This mysterious and elusive shadow often plays a strong role in untangling the ultimate meaning of the sacred dream.

Though Jung was openly scornful of organized religion, he did leave room for what I would regard a spiritual consciousness accessible through dreaming, in that he believed in archetypes of the soul. For him, the anima archetype represented the feminine side of a man's personality; and the animus, the masculine side of the female personality—though in some cases they could be portrayed by a figure of the same sex as the individual. Jung tended to analyze characters of the opposite sex in dreams as expressions of the anima or animus trying to tell us something about itself we need to know. He also believed that we tend to project our apprehensions and fears about our anima or animus soul-selves onto others. He used the example of a man reacting with ambivalence to women, regarding them as Madonnas or whores—a tendency that he believed could be recognized and healed through dream interpretation.

Though I am convinced anima and animus dream and mythological archetypes are real and have largely shaped gender attitudes throughout history, I do not associate them with the human soul in the same sense that Jung does. However, Jung does approach my concept of the soul-self that can be accessed in dreams in his description of the most fundamental archetype of Self, which he perceives as a merging of the many levels of the conscious and unconscious mind. He states that this archetype is often experienced as a transcendence into the totality of ultimate Self, which many people describe as the Divine or God.

One of the most significant contributions Jung made to the discipline of dream interpretation was his technique of amplification—a term he derived from the Latin *amplificatio*—a stage in the alchemical process. In *Psychology and Alchemy* he explains:

> The *amplificatio* is always appropriate when dealing with some obscure experience which is so vaguely adumbrated that it must be enlarged and expanded by being set in a psychological context in order to be understood at all. That is why, in analytical psychology, we resort to amplification in the interpretation of dreams, for a dream is too slender a hint to be understood until it is enriched by the stuff of association and analogy and thus amplified to the point of intelligibility.[20]

In essence, amplification is the process of isolating a symbolic image or sequence of events that occurred in a dream and removing it from the context of the dream scenario. Then the dream is consciously amplified by expanding the meaning of the dream symbol to discern other concepts or concerns the dreamer associates with it, and consequently what it signifies to the dreamer on a deeper psychological level. For example, if Jung was working with someone who dreamed of a snake, he would ask the dreamer to explain her experiences with the concept of a snake in general.

This method is different from Freud's method of free association in that it reaches deeper into the dreamer's conscious and unconscious ideas about a snake rather than focusing on words or ideas she has learned to relate to it. Whereas a Freudian free association list for "snake" might conjure up words like "slithery," "sneaky," or "frightening," Jung's method of amplification would challenge the dreamer to delve into her deeper consciousness and express what "snakeness" means to her, based on her own experience. Did she have nightmares about snakes slithering under her bed as a child? Had she been intrigued with snakes because of a close encounter she once had with one on a camping trip? Does she have a pet snake? One technique Jung would use to find out what a dreamer really thought about a dream symbol such as a snake was to ask her to pretend he had no idea what a snake was and to explain it to him in detail. In this manner, the dreamer would inadvertently relate what the essence of "snakeness" meant to her and probably relate valuable clues about what the snake signified within her dream.

Because Jung was convinced that humans can dream within the world of the collective unconscious, he also amplified the dream symbol by considering what it had traditionally stood for within the dreamer's cultural context. In addition, he researched how it had been used in ancient art, mythology, and lore in general. This was the method he used to decode the meaning of the young scientist's dreams. He amplified the recurring symbolism and realized it was strikingly similar to that used by ancient alchemists. This, in turn, led Jung to discover that the underlying meanings of the scientist's dreams were amazingly similar to the psychological aspects of the alchemists' endeavors, even though the scientist had no prior knowledge of the art of alchemy, much less its symbol system.

After a dream symbol had been amplified, Jung encouraged his clients to further their work with the dream image through a process he called active imagination. In a meditative state, the dreamer would focus on the dream image and observe how it progressed in movement or behavior while consciously trying not to mentally manipulate it in any way. In light of sacred dream practices we have examined from religious and cultural traditions throughout the world, this technique seems to honor the blurred line between sleeping and waking dream reality, although Jung would probably not have described it in this way.

COMMON RITUAL TECHNIQUES FOR SACRED AND PSYCHOLOGICAL DREAM INTERPRETATION

Interpreting a dream by analyzing its symbolism is a pervasive practice throughout the history of dream analysis. The metaphorical nature of dreams evidenced through symbolic imagery and literary wordplay is also universally recognized. While dream thought, as Jung said, is essentially undirected by language—because language is the basic symbol system that supports the entire system of symbols as they relate to one another and give meaning to the world—an undercurrent of linguistic awareness drives the metaphorical value of dreams. For example, upon hearing the word "rose," one automatically pictures a mental image of a rose and whatever the rose has come to signify for him, whether it is love, beauty, softness, or pain from being pricked by a thorn. So for an English speaker, the word "rose" is the fundamental symbol for "rose-ness." Interestingly enough, regardless of whether the dreamer is literate, during dreaming that takes the form of a story or narrative, the unconscious mind usually uses language as we hear it, rather than as we are accustomed to seeing it written. This is why a dream symbol often appears in the form of a pun or play on words. The image presented in the dream might be named by a word that is the same as or strikingly similar to the word the dreamer would associate with an image or concept that represents the true intent of the dream. One might dream of picking an actual rose, which on a deeper conscious level might signify his belief that he "rose" or could arise to some occasion.

This connection is especially prevalent in dreams when the deep conscious is trying to convey a message about a feeling, problem, or emotional concern for which there is no image that the dreamer normally associates with it. Rosemary Ellen Guiley, an expert on the occult, cites the example of a dream involving a bear, which might usually be associated with either ferocity and strength, or its archetypal image, protection. However, its presence might also indicate that the dreamer cannot bear something—in which case further symbolic analysis might indicate what that is. She also suggests that the appearance of a deer in a dream might signify something or someone who is dear to the dreamer, and a worn-out shoe could indicate that something is wearing down the dreamer's soul. Guiley remarks that when the deep meaning of a dream is based on a pun or a silly play on words, "it's as if the gods of dreaming have a great sense of humor."[21]

Modern depth psychology has shown that dream symbols can be generated from different levels of consciousness, some of which may actually transcend the personal cognitive experience of the dreamer and connect with humanity's archaic roots. Therefore, dream symbolism should be interpreted not only from the conscious awareness of the dreamer's waking life experience, but also from symbolic phenomena that affect the unconscious. These include the cultural contexts within which the dreamer lives and has lived, the mythology, lore, and artistic expression of the dreamer's immediate cultural milieu, and the entire spectrum of human history.

In working with spiritual dreamers and in instructing college courses on mythology, I have noticed an important aspect of dream interpretation that is rarely articulated and employed in historical methods, though it is often referred to. However, once it is purposely integrated into the method of dream analysis, new dimensions of dream meaning open up. The psychological architect and animator of unconscious symbolism is value. What we value most, what we are worried about or infatuated with, or, as Freud contends, what we wish for from within the depths of our souls will shape the symbol systems that populate our dreams.

Therefore, once a dream symbol or system of symbols is analyzed, the next step is to figure out how it fits into the dreamer's psyche in terms of what he values. The Chinese and the Mesopotamians interpreted their dreams as a means of obtaining what they valued most—to divine sacred knowledge about how to vanquish enemy forces or to prophesy how certain acts would affect future events. Jung's scientist discovered that his dream symbolism was guiding him toward what he valued most—rejuvenation and a sense of immortality.

As a final step in sacred dream interpretation, once the dream symbols have opened up the truth about the values the unconscious is trying to relate to the conscious psyche, the dreamer should take time to cognitively relate how these values have shaped her spiritual awareness and development, and how she wishes to increase or change these values to improve her life as a sacred dreamer.

Contemporary Sacred Dream Interpretation

Drawing from the techniques used in historical sacred dream interpretation of the world's religious traditions and those developed by modern depth psychologists, I have designed my four-step method for discerning the deep meaning of sacred dreams to deepen self-understanding and foster spiritual growth: (1) identify the prominent sacred symbols from your thick description dream journal of a dream narrative; (2) analyze the sacred symbols for their personal meaning, cultural meaning, and sacred meaning; (3) discern the values that underlie the symbols; and (4) relate these values to your spiritual awareness and development.

I developed the basis of this method for the sake of interpreting mythology in a college class I instruct, "Mythology, Value, and Culture." Throughout my own work with this method and that done by many students throughout the years, I can assert not only that it does work on anything that contains even a semblance of a story—including poetry, movies, and just about any form of art—but that if done with insight and care, it enables a multitude of new meanings to emerge from the narrative. I find that it is especially conducive to dream work, because, like mythology, which is essentially the dream consciousness of a culture, the core function of all personal dreams, even those that seem simple and straightforward, is always heavily shrouded in deep-conscious symbolism.

In order to illustrate the interworkings of each step of this method, I will apply it to the sacred feather dream I incubated earlier. The first step is to identify the sacred symbols from the dream narrative I wrote about in my journal with as much thick description as possible. I recorded my dream in this manner.

I was watching a fluffy white feather, falling, falling, falling in slow drifts, rocking gently back and forth in the air with a precision that struck me as though it had been purposely animated to do so. It fell for an inordinately long time in front of a sort of cliff or embankment covered with a dense growth of massive pine trees. As I watched the feather drift downward, I suddenly realized I was dreaming and that this was the dream I had incubated, though this was not the trim gray and white feather I had visualized when I did so. It also occurred to me within the dream that though I had pictured the dove's feather lying still at my feet while incubating this dream, in all the stories I had drawn upon when I decided to work with this

symbol, the way the feather had actually fallen into
each narrative experience had been an important
factor that I had not considered before. The backdrop
of pine trees seemed out of place.

I sensed within the dream that the feather knew
something I did not and had a sacred message to
impart. In this sense, I recognized that the feather
represented a sacred presence for me, so I asked it,
"Who are you?" At my request it twisted slightly
upward as it continued to fall and caught a shaft
of soft sunlight that subsided as quickly as it had
appeared. "Why are you falling?" I asked. At this
the feather gently landed on a bank of pure white
glistening snow and seemed to dissolve—white into
white. As I woke up, I realized I was cold.

Because the feather is the symbol I felt compelled to use to cultivate a sacred dream, obviously it is the symbol I should start with in interpreting the deep meaning of the dream. If I had had this dream without incubating it with the feather as a central symbol, I would still choose to analyze it, because it is the only active agent in the dream, save the wind it was riding on and my interaction with it. The fact that I sensed within the dream that it had a sacred message for me is also important. Other images I would analyze for symbolic content are the glint of sunlight through the feather, the pine trees, and the snow, because each of them struck me as sacred, curious, or out of place either within the dream itself or later while rehearsing it and writing in my journal about it.

The second step is to analyze each of the symbols for its meaning. Before I amplify each of the symbols I have identified as important or sacred, I relate the symbol system I have chosen from the general narrative of the dream to the events of my recent waking and dream life to see if I can draw any parallels between them. The dreaming consciousness often draws on the events and emotions of the previous day or two. With this dream I cannot remember any significant new information that preceded it except, of course, for the events in which a feather fell from the sky and into my life and the lives of the other two women who related similar stories. Then, of course, I had consciously affirmed that the feather may have sacred significance for me at this time in my life and I had decided to try to integrate the image into my sacred dream world in hopes that it would actually speak to me in some profound manner.

The feather that appeared in my dream was not the same as the image of the feather I incubated the dream with. But for the sake of listening to the message of the dream, I needed to amplify the feather symbol from the dream—especially because I lucidly realized the distinction within the dream itself. This amplification should be done with as much attention to detail as possible. The feather in the dream was pure white and fluffy, so temporarily removing this symbol from the dream, I start by asking myself what I automatically associate with a white, fluffy feather. Naturally I associate feathers in general with birds, and I entered the dream realm with this association. Because of the Christian culture within which I was raised, however, I realized that a feather like the one in the dream also brought back memories of Christmas pageants I had been in as a child and later produced as an adult in which I had assembled many angel costumes with wings of fluffy white feathers exactly like the one in my dream. I strongly associate this type of feather with birds and angels—beings that figuratively move about freely in the space between me and my culturally ingrained psychological assumption about where heaven is. Therefore, I can begin with the affirmation that within the makeup of my psychic experience, this feather is a message that bridges the gap between my human world and the heavenly world of the Divine, floating down with the intent of establishing a sacred connection or initiating sacred communication with me.

After deciding what the dream feather signified to me within the realm of my personal and cultural experience, the next important step is to look for clues about how it can be amplified from the perspective of what Jung calls the collective unconscious. But I prefer to think of as a sort of human-world consciousness. In other words, I do a little research into what this symbol has traditionally represented in mythology, lore, poetry, and visual art. I think through the mythology I am familiar with and remember the ancient Egyptians believed that when a person died, his soul was weighed against a single feather, the plume of Maat, who was the mother goddess of truth. In this case, the comparison with the feather reveals the weight or guilt of the human soul and the judgment of what the soul's afterlife will be like. Though this mythological feather story seems plausible in relation to my dream, it does not completely strike a chord of recognition within me, mostly because I have a strong sense that the feather in the dream did not signify a human soul. I continue to do more research.

In consulting a variety of books and websites about traditional and mythological symbolism, I also learn that shamans of many traditions equate the quality of the soul with the weight of a feather, and a light or pure soul can transcend the limitations of gravity, time, and space. The dream feather was falling toward the earth but in a way that did not seem bound by the laws of physical nature. The act of falling itself seemed to take place out of time, and I thought then that there was a tremendous feeling of spaciousness within the dream. The scene with the pine trees on the bluff behind the feather was absolutely panoramic.

Then I read that in ancient cultures, feathers were often associated with the concept of sacrifice, because when a bird was ritually slaughtered, a few feathers were left fluttering to the ground.[22] Something about this explanation strongly resonated with me, though I had no idea why at that time. I then remembered the reason I had gone outside in the first place the day the feather fluttered to my feet—to pray for an acquaintance who had passed away. Trusting my own instincts, I began to piece together the deep-conscious values that this dream feather was trying to relate. I realized it was conveying repressed feelings of sacrifice.

When I considered possible linguistic symbols of my dream feather, my heart felt like it froze. The word "feather" is strikingly similar to the name of a person involved in a situation I had been going through at the time that had caused me a great sense of loss and sacrifice. Everything about the dream and my decision to incubate sacred dream activity with this particular symbol started to make sense. That my unconscious would code the situation involving this individual stood to reason, because the feather represented the huge problem that had been absorbing my energy and attention, but I had worked hard to suppress it from my conscious waking life because of all the pain and anger it triggered within me. When the conscious mind evades a psychic problem, however, the unconscious continues to try to work it out and find a way to re-present it to the consciousness, so it might finally be resolved. Thus, in Freudian terms, my unconscious mind "disguised" my heartache and loss by presenting it in the form of a word that sounded similar and slipped it back into my waking and sleeping dream consciousness.

Further amplification of the symbol system of this dream shows that it did more than just force me to confront my deepest feelings about this problem, however. It offered sacred wisdom and consolation. Despite the linguistic twist substituting the word "feather" for the name of a specific person, I still somehow knew that the feather itself, though calling to mind this situation, did not represent any actual soul, or person, or even the situation itself—which I felt was signified by the overwhelming vastness of the scene and by the sense of timelessness imbuing it.

In amplifying the manner in which the feather was falling, I considered that, from my own previous sacred dream work, I had learned that when I have dreams about falling, they usually occur because I feel as though I am losing control of some aspect of my life. Though the situation the feather is representing is one in which I do feel desperately out of control, I now know that the feather is not signifying that I am falling. In fact, in my journal I noted specifically that it seemed as though someone was "animating" the fall of the feather. Therefore, though my psyche still associates the sensation of falling with a lack of personal control, in this instance, the feather is being controlled by someone or something else, and who but the Divine could control the airflow in which a feather falls? It was bringing sacred enlightenment about the situation, but the sacred message of the dream was encoded in the other symbols that framed the action of the feather falling.

After amplifying the other symbols I had chosen for analysis in the same manner as I had the feather, I concluded that the way the light glimmered through the form of the feather after I had lucidly asked it who it was confirmed that it was the Divine—which I have come to strongly associate with pure light. The reason the background was framed by a massive growth of pine trees in the dream is that pine trees are evergreens—a perennial symbol of strength, fertility, hope, and immortality. The curious appearance of snow on the ground as the feather alighted, coupled with the sensation of cold I experienced upon waking and compounded by the feeling that my heart froze when I realized the core truth about the feather's significance, I understand as the chill of realization that accompanies confrontation with something painful that I have been repressing. The scene did not take place on a completely bleak snowy day, however. The sun glinted through the feather, and I had noted in my journal entry the glittering purity of the snow as well as the whiteness of the feather.

The underlying value of this dream, which I firmly believe was a sacred gift sent to me at my request and intended to bear me up through a difficult situation, was that of hope—encoded in the evergreen trees and the glittering effects of the sun through the feather and on the surface of the snow. I described the way the feather melted into the snow when it landed as "white on white." White signifies purity and innocence. The fact that it seemed to dissolve into the snow to the point where it became almost indistinguishable I strongly sensed was a sacred prophecy that if I regarded the painful aspects of this situation with patience, faith, and purity of heart, they would eventually fade away.

I could have stopped here with a great sense of peace and contentment. But because I have come to regard the art of sacred dreaming as a spiral that has no end, I have continued to take the imprint of this dream symbolism into my waking and dreaming life. For example, I had been searching for the perfect soulful venue in which to lead some retreats close to home. After looking at several locations, I visited one that had been built by a woman who was an artist and a healer. As we left the meeting space that had been her home, my guide pointed out a small circular shadow-box window next to the entrance to the back porch. Within it was a large grayish-white feather the owner had deemed to be of sacred significance. I caught my breath. The feather was a perfect amalgamation of the one that had fallen to my feet, which I had used to incubate my sacred dream, and the one that had appeared in the dream. Though some minor complications with the property had to be worked through, I knew I had received sacred confirmation that this was where I needed to conduct my retreats.

I have also used my dream feather in the cultivation of more sacred dreaming with astounding results, which unfortunately are too involved to include here. This deep sacred dream work opens the way to new realms of spiritual growth, however, and therefore I honored the symbolic wisdom that had already developed throughout the sacred dreaming process. I then incubated later dreams by concentrating on the newly encoded sacred symbolism of the feather's slight imprint melting into the glistening snow.

Discerning the Deep Meaning of Sacred Dreams

As you interpret the sacred messages that arise from your deep conscious, keep a couple of guiding rules in mind. No doubt as you become more aware of your dream life, you will also remember more dreams. Dream interpretation can be a long and thoughtful process, so when this happens, rehearsing, recording, and analyzing all your dreams becomes impossible within normal life. You will have to select those that seem to hold the most promise for spiritual growth and self-understanding. The first guiding principle of sacred dream work, however, is not to neglect to interpret a significant dream because it does not immediately seem to be sacred. Some of the dreams that have the most powerful sacred messages are often so subtly encoded in metaphor that their spiritual content only spills out during interpretation. Remembering that Bulkeley's survey showed that most people found that their big or most profoundly memorable dreams were also those they considered mystical, a good rule of thumb is to analyze any dream that seems especially profound or memorable as if it is a sacred dream. With analysis, it will almost always turn out to be so. If you are a spiritual person, most of your dreams will contain spiritual messages.

Another critical rule to keep in mind throughout your sacred dream work is to trust your instincts. I echo Artemidorus, who warned the Greeks that personal experience is the only true interpreter of dreams. Whether the symbols and events that occur in your dreams are of personal, cultural, world-consciousness, or even divine origin, everything that appears in your dreams works within the different levels of your own consciousness. I have no doubt that many people who read my interpretation of my sacred feather dream would be confused about why I chose one symbolic interpretation over another, for at many turns, I obviously could have chosen otherwise. But the true work of sacred dream interpretation is as emotionally driven as the dream itself, because the content of our dreams, especially our sacred dreams, is based in our own deepest personal needs, concerns, and desires. For this reason, when you are trying to decide among possible meanings for the symbol or aspect of the dream you are analyzing, you can trust your gut completely. The ones that evoke an "aha" experience or emotional response are the ones that hold the true intent of the dream. Though discussing your dreams with a friend, relative, or even an analyst may produce insights, in the long run, you are the only one who can effectively interpret your sacred dreams.

1. Identify the prominent sacred symbols in your dream.

Reread your thick description journal entry, and highlight or underline any symbols that seem to you to be supercharged with significance. Symbolic dream imagery can take the shape of any object, form, color, number, or even feeling. It can be either a clear or an indiscernible presence (remember Jung's psychologized selves). What is more, even the smallest dream sequence can be packed with significant metaphor. Because unraveling the meaning of just one dream symbol can turn out to be a lengthy (though always fascinating) process, the task is to decide which symbols carry the greatest sacred dream significance and are therefore worth analyzing in depth.

For the sake of interpreting sacred dreams, you would of course focus on any symbol or cluster of symbols that you sense are charged with sacred essence within the dream or that began to emerge as spiritually charged while rehearsing or writing in a journal about the dream. If the spiritual imagery in the dream is not directly evident, yet you feel the dream was somehow sacred, pick out any symbols that recur, remembering that the mind tends to use repetition as a means of emphasis. In addition, be sure to flag any symbols or symbolic sequences in the dream that strike you as particularly curious or odd or that seem to be so foreign in mental or emotional impact that you think they could not have been generated from within your own mind.

2. Analyze the sacred symbols.

If you write your dream journal on the left side of a double-page or double-column format, use the right side to note the meaning of the symbols as you figure them out. I like to use a different color of ink or a different font so the distinction between the dream and the dream work is obvious at a glance. After I have analyzed the important symbols, I use a third color to write my conclusions about the sacred dream in general. However you choose to structure your work, analyze each symbol for its personal meaning, its cultural or world-consciousness meaning, and its sacred meaning.

Beginning with your personal dream symbol analysis, ask yourself if the symbol, within or outside the context of the whole dream, relates in any way to something you have witnessed, thought about, or experienced within the past day or so. The dreaming mind has a tendency to pick up traces of recent conscious awareness that it feels need more examination or resolution. Then, considering the symbol separately from the context of the dream, ask yourself what from your personal experience you automatically tend to associate with that particular symbol. Ask yourself whether it might somehow represent an aspect of yourself. Consider whether the symbol represents a pun or play on words for another image or concept, and do not neglect to evaluate any paradox—an opposite meaning or "shadow of intent"—that it might represent. Make note of any emotions or sudden realizations that this symbol might invoke.

Consider cultural associations you connect with the symbol— whether they are communal on a small scale, regional, religious, or even concepts you may have adopted from mass media. Think about anything you have read, art you have seen, fairy or folktales you were raised with, or mythology you are familiar with that may contain your symbol. Then check a good sourcebook or website for traditional symbolism (I have listed a couple of my favorites in "Suggestions for Further Reading") to see if any of the ancient interpretations of your symbol resonate with the way it appeared in your dream sequence. Again, make note of any clues you find that seem to speak to your dream.

Look through your dream journal and consider how your dream symbol or symbol system relates to other dreams you have had. Thoughtful dream work will show that meaningful symbolic patterns not only emerge from within one dream, but will span a number of dreams. Making the connections can produce astounding results. After you have analyzed all the significant symbols in your dream, any sacred content of your dream that was not evident from the start should begin to manifest itself. Take time to write in your journal about how that is taking shape and how you feel about it.

3. Discern the values that underlie the symbols.

If you have performed a thoughtful and resourceful analysis of the sacred symbols in your dream, the underlying values will naturally surface. Just as my need for a glimmer of hope in a difficult situation and for assurance that the Divine was in control of it when I felt so powerless was answered within my own sacred dream, you will discover that values will materialize from yours, so it pays to be mindful of them. And, even more importantly, acknowledge the deep values that are driving your sacred dreams. I had repressed my feelings about this situation to the point that I did not consciously realize I was longing for divine intervention and hope. The dream not only pointed out what holes need to be filled in my own unconscious in order to heal and go forward with my life more holistically, but also assured me that I had sacred support in the process. Identifying and acknowledging the core values that drive the sacred dream symbolism is the key to using the sacred art of dreaming as a means of personal and spiritual growth.

4. Relate these values to your spiritual awareness and development.

Many elements of the sacred relevance of your dream may have become obvious by this point in the interpretation. But whether or not they have, take a few moments to think about how the values that generated the symbolism within your dream relate to the general direction in which your spiritual life seems to be going in your waking life. Because our core values are also those that shape our religious practices and spiritual quests, awareness of those values that have been languishing in the unconscious can be enlightening.

Above all, honor whatever sacred presence, communication, or awareness you have been blessed with through dream work by taking it forward into your spiritual life. Be aware of how the symbol system that shaped your sacred dream continues to speak to you in mysterious and wonderful ways during your waking life experience. If you feel that a sacred presence or other form of spiritual communication within your dream was compelling you to act in a particular manner in your waking life, follow through—whether this entails further thought, prayer, communicating something to another person, or some sort of community involvement or activism. Honor the sacred messages that bless you in your dreams.

In addition, be sure to take symbols that have developed within your dream interpretations into your future dreams as pre-sleep incubation signs. With consistency and determination to recognize the continuity of sacred activity throughout all levels of your consciousness, your sacred dream work will surely spiral into untold new dimensions of meaning and enrichment.

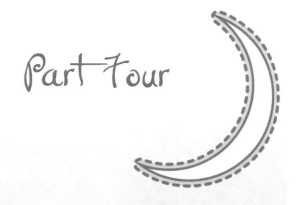

Part Four

Sacred Dream Work as a Means of Personal Fulfillment and Spiritual Growth

CHAPTER SEVEN

SACRED DREAMING AND THE CREATION OF SACRED ART

Without a doubt, the ultimate manner in which a human can emulate the Divine is through the act of creation. Any artwork—whether a painting, a poem, a dance, or a song—is an emotive interaction with some aspect of creation. Those who are spiritually centered can fully appreciate the sacred relationship between the divine creator and human creation. Clarissa Pinkola Estés, who describes herself as a *cantadora,* or keeper of the old stories in the Latin tradition, has mesmerized her readers by retelling sacred stories with the aid of a vast array of creative visual art and poetry. I like the way she describes the soul's need for creative expression:

> Some say the creative life is in ideas, some say it is in doing. It seems in most instances to be in a simple being. It is not virtuosity, although that is very fine in itself. It is the love of something, having so much love for something—whether a person, a word, an image, an idea, the land, or humanity—that all that can be done with the

overflow is to create. It is not a matter of wanting to, not
a singular act of will; one solely must.[1]

From this perspective, I see the creation of art based on sacred
dreams as an overflow of love for the relationship between the
dreamer and the Divine, as it is experienced by the dreamer
within waking and sleeping consciousness. The sacred dream
artistic process indicates a yearning to understand this relationship as fully as possible, to enrich it and share the joy that
it brings anyone who might be in a position to appreciate it.

All people who have spent a great deal of time at any craft
have had to grapple with the reality that the life of an artist
can be quite lonely. Perhaps the greatest gift of sacred dream
art creation is that it is a collaborative experience, and consequently the fruition of a project becomes a shared triumph.
What is more, creative collaboration with the Divine brings
out the very essence of a human's personality, gifts, and talents.
Through active, conscious participation with the act of divine
creation, as it is revealed to your inner psychic nature through
dreams, one can fully experience what Aristotle called *eudemo-
nia,* or the fullest expression of human happiness, good spirit,
and flourishing.

DREAM WORK AND ARTWORK

The integral relationship between human dreaming and creative artwork is much more profound than most people probably realize. Some of the world's most notable artists generated
their work from the overflow of creative influence, imagery,
and energy they received within their dreams. In his book *Our
Dreaming Mind,* psychologist Robert L. Van de Castle presents
a rather astounding list of artists of various mediums whose
works have been patronized by their dreams. Among the visual
artists is Salvador Dalí, who became fascinated with dreams

after reading Freud's *Interpretation of Dreams* and came to think of his works as "hand-painted dream photographs." The visionary artist and poet William Blake drew the portrait of the man who taught him painting in his dreams. French sculptor Jean Dupre's *Pieta* was fashioned in imitation of the way it appeared to him within a dreamscape, though he later admitted he felt he had failed to produce it with the grandeur with which he had dreamt it.

The Swedish filmmaker Ingmar Bergman took great pains in his movies to reproduce episodes from his dreams as accurately as possible. The American actor and director Orson Wells said that he based the dreamlike quality of his film *The Trial* on one of his dreams, and Italian director Franco Fellini fashioned his grotesque and surreal characters on those that had appeared in his mind as he slept. In 1902, Nobel Prize winner William Butler Yeats wrote the play *Cathleen ni Houlihan* based on a woman who had come to him in his dreams. Mary Shelley's *Frankenstein* was written after a nightmare, as was Robert Louis Stevenson's *The Strange Case of Dr. Jekyll and Mr. Hyde.* Other authors who relied on the authority of their dreams in producing some of their greatest works include Franz Kafka, Katherine Mansfield, and Charlotte Brontë. Poets Voltaire, John Masefield, Johann von Goethe, and Christina Rossetti also claimed that they drew creatively on their dreams.[2]

The musician and dream educator Nancy Grace proclaims that contemporary musicians who find inspiration in their dreams share a spiritual lineage with indigenous and shamanic peoples who have traditionally relied on their dreams for their creative spiritual powers. In her essay "Making Dreams into Music," she recognizes several contemporary songwriters and musicians whom she believes are spiritual descendants of ancient dreamers, including Sting, who on a radio interview once said he thought that "any artist who ignores their dreams is ignoring half their creative potential." When performer Billy Joel spoke at Berklee College of Music in Boston and was asked where he gets his ideas for songs, he responded that all of them come from dreams. Paul McCartney dreamt the melody for the Beatles hit song "Yesterday."[3]

SACRED ARTWORK AS PART OF THE SACRED DREAM SPIRAL

Creating sacred dream artwork is an especially high and noble calling as well as an important part of the sacred dream spiral, because it honors the relationship between the human and the Ultimate Reality you encounter in dreams as a perpetual process of love, renewal, and growth. Whether the dreaming artist pours out his love in the form of visual arts such as drawing, painting, photography, mosaic, fiber arts, or sculpting; in literary art forms such as poetry or prose; in dance or other movement; or in music or drama, the process is cocreative. The energy expended is shared, the intent is exchanged, and the finished product is a tangible expression of a loving relationship. In all, it deepens that relationship in a remarkably satisfying manner.

Sacred artwork is particularly conducive to sacred dream work, because it is not dependent on the conventions of language, which allows the dreamer more freedom to imitate the quality of the sacred dream content. Even in the case of writing poetry, creative prose, musical lyrics, or a dramatic script, the artistic progression is driven more by the remembrance of the dreamscape, the clusters of meaning and events, and the emotional impact of its content than writing that is done with normal waking intention. In short, writing and all other forms of art that are produced from dreaming can come from all the levels of consciousness that can access our minds in dream. In comparing dreams to ecstatic mystical experiences, the Mayan shaman Barbara Tedlock explains it in this way:

> These intense sensory experiences—so difficult to describe in words—are also related to a combination of brain symmetry and chemistry. During ecstatic mystical experiences the image-based right hemisphere of the brain comes to dominate the left hemisphere, where most language processing takes place. Mystical states, like dreams, are fundamentally nonlinear, nonlinguistic, and distorted beyond recognition when put into words or conveyed to others. This is why many people are reticent when asked to describe their visions and why many others prefer to draw, paint, or weave key images from these experiences rather than attempt to directly talk about them.[4]

Because sacred artwork based on sacred dreaming tends to take the artist back into the conscious mode of the dream for an extended period of time, it is a powerful field for dream amplification. A myriad of symbolic details—colors, shapes, numbers, sounds, expressive movements, and the like—that are purposely or inadvertently included in the execution of the work of art are fair game for further dream analysis. All sorts of new meaning can suddenly pop up during the process and can be included in a dream journal and used as intentional symbolism to incubate a whole new level of sacred dream experience and awareness. I think of this process as a sacred dream–sacred art feedback loop. From my own experience and those of dreamers who have shared their sacred dream–sacred art experiences with me, I have found that creating sacred dream art within sacred dream work not only opens up the process to a different level, but also fosters a deepening sense of communion with the Divine at a rate and level that is exponentially superior to what was experienced before.

Converting the Sacred Dream
into Waking Life Sacred Art

The manner in which you approach the creation of art is a matter of personal preference. For this reason as well as that fact that an artist might perform her sacred artwork in such a wide range of artistic mediums, I would not presume to guide you through the particulars of your own sacred art endeavor. I can offer, however, a few tested guidelines on how to integrate your process of creating sacred artwork into the art of sacred dream work in such a way that both might be enhanced.

Which of your dreams you choose to render in art is also a matter of personal choice; however, I would suggest trying to work creatively with any dream that you sense is particularly big, powerful, or memorable, especially if it has an apparent sacred character. In rare but wonderful cases, a dreamer might be gifted in a dream with an art masterpiece in its perfect entirety and upon waking feel immediately compelled to execute it. If this should happen to you, by all means follow through as your heart dictates. But in all other cases, I recommend spending some time reading through your journal about the particular dream you plan to immortalize in art. Even though the written word cannot convey the full emotional impact of the actual dream, because your own consciousness originally dreamed it, your notes on it should help to place you mentally and emotionally back into the original dreamscape.

1. Ritualize and savor the sacred dream art process.

I find that the best way to reach a sleeping dream conscious state while awake is to enter into the act of creation of art with the same honor and intent with which I enter into dream space. As in any human undertaking, the intensity with which you will experience the fruits of the process depends on the intensity of the honor with which you approach it. Start by establishing your workspace as a creative dream art temple. Though this could itself be a huge undertaking, it can be as simple as blessing your workspace, assembling a small shrine nearby, or taking a few moments to sense that you and your space are filling with sacred creative energy. Gather up whatever you will need for your art project, being mindful to integrate each tool or raw material into the spiritually charged temple of creation you have formed. This can be done with spatial placement or simply with a few moments of mental acknowledgment. Do not forget to include your sacred dream journal—open to the dream you are working with. The objective is to infuse the area and everything you will touch with sacred vitality.

I always light a candle and recite a prayer or invocation before I begin. Just as the ancients consistently used fire as a sacred ritual element to guide the waking mind into the realm of sacred dreams, you will find that fire will have the same effect as you consciously try to shift your mind from waking cognitive consciousness into a state that is more similar to your sleeping sacred dream consciousness while executing your sacred art. The leaping of a flame as it takes the energy of the air is highly symbolic of inspiration that is fueled by Spirit. It is a pervasive archetypal motif, and its imprint on the world-consciousness level of the psyche should not be underestimated. Dream artists who ritually tend a candle or fire while they work often find that it comes to signify the presence of the Divine throughout the process.

After lighting a candle or tending a fire near your creative workspace, offer up a prayer in whatever manner helps you to focus on the relationship between yourself and the sacred dream presence or communication you will explore with your art as well as your intention to honor and deepen that relationship. From this extemporaneous prayer, distill a few words or a short phrase that sums up your intention for the sacred art you will create and to use as a meditative mantra or focus. For me, the few moments of prayer form the portal of consciousness through which I approach the sacred dream world where my work will take place.

At this point, settle into this magical realm of consciousness through meditative breathing. I suggest using the same basic technique used for cultivating sacred dreams, with minor alterations for sacred dream artwork. Sit in a comfortable position with your spine fully extended. Take a deep, comfortable breath and feel it filling your whole body with soft, bright light. Hold the breath momentarily before exhaling slowly. Repeat breathing in this manner as you continue to mentally recite your sacred dream art intention.

Preparation for sacred artwork itself can be a highly creative act of personal self-expression. Feel free to change any of these suggestions or integrate other ritual elements that might work better for you from your own experience or in honor of your own religious tradition. Make sure, however, that whatever ritual process you use to prepare for your sacred dream artwork has strong parallels to those you use in cultivating your sacred dreams. This is the surest way to condition your consciousness to access the deeper levels with which it dreams and to ensure the flow and continuity of the sacred spiral of your dream work.

2. Begin execution of your sacred dream art by staying true to the sacred dream content.

When during your meditative breathing you feel you are relaxed and focused, take up your journal and read thoughtfully through your account of the dream and any interpretive notes you have made on it. When you feel yourself consciously entering the dreamscape, begin your work. Initially, create from the emotion of the dream. That is, whether you feel compelled to base your artistic work on a certain scene, sequence, or symbol of the dream, respond to it instead of replicating it. Instead of choosing a symbol or scene, let it choose you. Instead of selecting a color from your palette, let it select you. Instead of instigating a movement, let it move you. Instead of finding the right word to describe it, let the right word find you.

Staying true to the original integrity of the dream is perhaps the most difficult part of generating art for the sake of responding to and perpetuating the flow of sacred dream awareness and growth. We are used to approaching the creation of art with the intention, in part, of producing something that will have enough aesthetic finesse that it can be displayed and appreciated by the public and throughout posterity. I am not saying this cannot be the ultimate aim of your sacred dream artwork. As we have seen, some of the world's most valued masterpieces were generated from dreams. Still, I highly recommend that you begin your work of art in a psychic state of complete surrender to the dream content itself. After you have finished it to your satisfaction, record it by taking a photograph of it, filming it, or using whatever manner of preservation is appropriate to your artistic medium, and then put that record into your dream journal adjacent to your notes on the dream itself.

You may be fortunate enough that the art you have created from a pure response to your dream is such that it is ready for public presentation. If not, you can certainly continue work on it or use it as a basis for further art projects that may well produce a masterful result. For example, I felt compelled to mold in plaster and paint with acrylics my fluffy white feather as it melted into the sparkling snow from my previous dream—going so far as to add iridescent highlights to accurately portray the strength of the imagery in the dream and the emotional impact it had on me. In my original dream piece, the feather is so well dissolved into the snow, it is almost imperceptible. Visually, the work was so monochromatic and shiny that I had no doubt it would hold no aesthetic value for anyone but me. Nonetheless, it pleased me in that it perfectly captured the essence of the dream symbolism in such a way that I could respond to it, further my dream analysis with it, find deeper sacred significance in the dream work, and take it back into my future sacred dreams with more awareness and refined intent. I took a photograph of it, put the photo in a plastic sleeve, inserted it into my dream journal, and later painted more contrast and definition into the work. Though the final result is not something that would ever be placed in an art gallery, it did turn out to have enough grace and character that I was proud to include it in one of the many sacred shrines that continue to almost magically materialize around my home and workspace.

For many sacred dream professional artists, time and the cost of materials might inhibit the ability to generate dream art separately from art they must create and distribute as their livelihood. If this is the case for you, to nurture the work of your sacred dream spiral, make an effort throughout the process of creating your dream artwork to be aware of what you are doing in direct response to the dream itself and what you are adding, taking away, accentuating, or minimizing for the sake of public presentation or consumption.

Understanding the psychic levels of dream consciousness not only explains why the art generated from it works differently on a personal level from art other people can appreciate, but also gives the sacred dream artist valuable insights into how to create art that more people can respond to on a deeper level. Remember that dreams are made up of psychologized information from personal, cultural, and world-consciousness levels and that sacred dreams may also contain special input directly from the Divine. Furthermore, dreams that have a sacred character often draw on all levels simultaneously. Therefore, it stands to reason that the artwork generated from a sacred dream would be designed and encoded by the different levels of the dreamer's particular consciousness. Someone who masters the art of sacred dream interpretation soon learns to identify the difference between these psychic levels. When this becomes possible, the dreamer can more readily recraft the sacred dream artwork he intends to share by accentuating the elements of the dream's story and metaphor that are recognizable as archetypal symbols of human core values—or those that are shared on a cultural or world level of consciousness.

As a published sacred dream poet, I can best illustrate how this works by drawing on my own experience creating dream poetry and the methods I use to adapt it for publication. I write the first draft of my poem in direct response to sacred dream content, as described here. I further revise and edit the poem until I am satisfied that it contains the full expression of the sacred content of the dream and is aesthetically pleasing to me. I put a copy of this poem in my dream journal. If I feel this particular poem has a message I would like to share with the world at large, I revise it for publication.

The first step in this revision process is to make sure the poem carries an underlying story that is based on the core values I have extrapolated from the dream. Core values are almost always universally shared. If the dream story is so convoluted that I feel no one else would be able to follow it, I connect the dots between the clusters of symbols to the point that I feel most readers could grasp the meaning. Then I refine it by minimizing or eliminating the dream symbolism and content that I recognize has originated from my personal consciousness and by emphasizing or adding dream symbolism and content that I am sure drew on archetypal or cultural content—especially what I perceive as world-consciousness symbolism. Continued revision and editing usually produces a poem that most people can identify with—at least unconsciously, if not immediately on a cognitive level. However, if enough of the archetypal metaphor within the poem is presented with the emotional quality of the dream itself, it should evoke enough of an unconscious response that the reader will be willing to study it further to discover the underlying story and to experience the emotional impact of the human and sacred values that drive it. In my opinion, truly fine art leads an observer on a mystical adventure through his own levels of consciousness, which should be almost as intriguing and awe-inspiring as the one the artist took when she created it.

3. Amplify any new symbolism that arises from the creation of your sacred art.

New symbols with potent spiritual energy commonly just appear in creative artwork based on a sacred dream. They may take the form of something the artist felt compelled to add. Oftentimes, when an artist takes another look at his artwork later—perhaps as his consciousness reverts back to more of a normal waking consciousness, they may suddenly become evident, although the artist had no idea he was integrating them into the work. For example, in seminars I have led, we often design mandalas based on our deep-conscious dream work. One participant drew a succession of shapes and colors and later realized she had imposed a huge lemniscate (figure eight) over the other forms in her drawing. Because this is the symbol for infinity, further dream analysis opened up a whole new arena of meaning for her sacred dream. Another participant drew a figure of herself with her arms raised, which she interpreted as an expression of joy and self-transcendence. Upon later inspection, however, she realized that the way the figure was drawn, surrounded by two huge whorls of color, made it look remarkably like a huge butterfly. Even though these dream artists had no intention to draw lemniscates or butterflies, and had no awareness of the fact that they were doing so, the symbols that emerged could be considered as important as those that were added intentionally, because the unconscious has a magical and mysterious way of speaking to the consciousness in disguised clues and riddles.

Even in art forms that are not visual, new symbols are sure to be generated from executing the work, and these should be analyzed with as much care as those that arose within the dreamscape. Use the same methods to analyze them in the sacred dream practice "Discerning the Deep Meaning of Sacred Dreams" in chapter 6.

4. Record your artwork and dream-artwork interpretation in your dream journal.

You should understand by now why I recommended earlier that you use a loose-leaf binder or electronic filing system to which you can keep adding files as you continue your sacred dream journey. Sacred dream work can become as elusive as dreams themselves.

Every act of energy and awareness you spend on a sacred dream will usually further your spiritual understanding to some extent, however. In time, when you look back through your journal at a body of work you did on a certain dream, it can speak to you in a completely new way. Above all, keeping a journal and interpreting the symbolism of your sacred artwork not only will ensure continuity in your sacred dream life, but will enable you to experience the magical quality of the dream world in your waking life as well.

5. Integrate your sacred artwork back into the sacred dream process.

Just as the feather encased in the wall of the retreat center struck me with a sense of awe and clarity because of my sacred feather dream spiral, you might be amazed at how the symbol amplification from your dream artwork begins to speak to you within your everyday life. If you have honored the sacred relationship during the sacred dream art creation process by bringing the symbol from the unconscious to the conscious and decoding its sacred message, then the sacred communion of that work will undoubtedly continue to influence your conscious awareness within your waking and sleeping experiences.

Nurture the growth of this sacred dream spiral by taking any dream symbols you have already been working with that have progressed during your sacred dream artwork, any new symbols that might have emerged from it, and any new amplification and journal writing you have done back into your dream world as a symbol for incubating new sacred dreams. Make a conscious effort to be aware of how every step of this process opens your mind, heart, and soul to the spiritual reality that works within and around you.

CHAPTER EIGHT

THE ART OF SACRED
DREAM HEALING

As evidenced by the tremendous cult of Asclepius in Greece and Rome, the arts of sacred dreaming and healing have been associated throughout the history of humankind.

Drawing on a sample of over 100,000 dreams, theology professor and professional dream worker Jeremy Taylor claims that he has not heard a single dream or had an experience working with a dream that has not contributed to his conviction that "all dreaming is deeply involved with health and wholeness, not just of the individual dreamer, but the entire species."[1] As embodied entities of energy and spirit, the deep-conscious levels of our minds are always trying to understand how physical, psychological, and spiritual energies (often understood as the soul) are coping with their confinement within the body and working to keep these energies balanced. This is the sacred work of dreams.

DREAMING AS A MEANS OF PHYSICAL HEALING

Embodiment is a huge aspect of dreaming. As we are shifting from waking to dreaming consciousness, the input of the world at large is quieting down and the boundaries of the energies that make up the self become more obvious. The dreaming mind responds to these boundaries in two basic ways. It either focuses on the nature and quality of the self within these boundaries, or it challenges the boundaries of embodiment by experimenting with means of transcending those boundaries, resulting in some sort of out-of-body experience. Dreaming with sacred or spiritual awareness greatly enhances both. It can lend the introspective-body dream a spiritual observer who conveys the inner workings of its energy balance. In addition, the limits of embodiment tend to seem more permeable for one who dream-travels in the form of her spiritual or soul-self.

Patricia Garfield, internationally recognized authority on dreams, advanced a basic theory of physical dream healing by examining her own dreams throughout the physical trauma and healing she experienced as a result of breaking her wrist. In her book *The Healing Power of Dreams*, she asserts that "peering through the windows of our dreams, we can watch our bodies at work."[2] She believes that dreams broadcast nightly bulletins about your health that serve as news flashes that are critical for your well-being.[3] Learning to recognize these dreams can be a vital means of maintaining a holistic balance of physical, mental, and spiritual health. The best way to recognize and honor these dreams, Garfield says, is to learn to identify the personal metaphors and symbols that your dreaming mind tends to use to represent your body, your ill health, your good health, and changes in your health.

In dreams, the most common metaphors for bodies are buildings (often houses) and vehicles. Because buildings have a definite inside and outside, these dreams often represent the condition or feeling of being confined within our body. The nature or condition of the building usually reflects the condition of the self that the dream is dealing with. So dreams of houses or homes often indicate the condition of your body. Dreaming of a dilapidated home might indicate feelings of being physically exhausted, run down, or beaten up. On the other hand, dreams that take place inside a skyscraper or office complex might reflect the condition of your physical body in relation to the society in which you are involved.

The condition of the building parts commonly serves as metaphors for the condition, or change in condition, for specific parts of the human body. Garfield notes some commonplace examples of this. The condition of the staircase can suggest the condition of the dreamer's spine. A dream about a staircase with rotten steps might signal spinal degeneration, whereas a dream about a beautiful, strong, glowing staircase might signify robust spinal health or perhaps even the metaphorical ability to stand up straight and proud. Other frequent building-body metaphors include an association between the framework and the skeleton, the windows and the eyes, the furnace and the stomach or the womb, the plumbing and the blood vessels, and the electrical wiring and the nerves. Additionally, the overall condition of the dream building or house can indicate the dreamer's current lifestyle or attitude.[4]

Dreams about vehicles also often represent the dreamer's conceptualization of embodied self, but whereas building dreams tend to convey hints about the condition of the body, vehicle dreams are more apt to reflect the dreamer's unconscious feelings about how much control he has over his body or the direction in which his life is heading. The type of vehicle most dreamt about has historically mirrored the most popular forms of transportation used within a particular culture. Not surprisingly, today the most common dream vehicle is the automobile, a word that Garfield reminds us is derived from the Greek *autos,* meaning "self," and the Latin *mobilis,* or "mobile." The linguistic tie between the human as an embodied self and its movement through time, space, or life in general carries over

into the metaphorical nature of dreaming. The deep consciousness senses the correspondence between an automobile and the
human body even when the waking consciousness fails to see
it. Both entities require energy input and the output of waste.
Both require regular maintenance to function well. Both are
prone to accidents and breakdowns, and both can go too fast,
too slow, or just right.[5]

Car parts that frequently advise the dreamer of parallel
issues concerning body movement or control include the steering wheel, which can indicate the dreamer's mind-set about
control of direction; the brakes, which can intimate feelings
about the level of control you have over bodily function or life
situation; and the engine or other concealed mechanisms that
can signal issues with inner organs. Other common automobile dream metaphors are associations between the body of the
car and the human body surface, the headlights and the eyes or
ability to see—physically or metaphorically—the horn and the
voice or power of voice, the fuel and energy level, and the tires
or wheels and the legs.[6] When analyzing a vehicle dream for
the sake of healing, you should also always ask, "Who is doing
the driving?"

Particularly astounding about all of this is that when our
bodies are becoming ill or disturbed, or are malfunctioning in
any way, our unconscious usually has access to this information
before our consciousness does. Consequently, as Garfield says,
"Our dreams are often the first to know." She maintains that if
we learn to decode the information in our dreams about distur-
bances in our normal body function, they often show us the exact
location of the disturbance, the symptoms of the disturbance, and
the malfunctioning involved in the disturbance, and in many
instances before the waking consciousness gets the hint that anything is wrong.[7] In this respect, conscientious attention to your
dreams may be one of the best preventative remedies available.

DREAMING AS A MEANS OF PSYCHOLOGICAL HEALING

Anthropologist Douglas Hollan agrees that "many people may dream of damage or repair to their brains or bodies long before such injury or repair becomes manifest in physical or behavioral symptoms."[8] He refers to dreams about the inner workings of the self as "selfscape" dreams, and claims that they provide a vantage point from which we can observe how our minds continually update and map out the self's current state of affairs. Hollan takes the concept of the healing power of dreams one step further in saying that selfscape dreams not only relate the status of the self as a mental and biological entity, but also reflect the relations of the self to other objects and people. Hence, selfscape dreams reflect the psychological and emotional ramifications of the perceived social status of the dreamer, and in turn, are often shaped by cultural ideas about society and social status.[9] Thus, paying careful attention to our dreams can help us to take better care of our physical health, as well as our emotional health as it is related to our relationships and social standing.

LaBerge and Rheingold agree that dreaming, especially lucid dreaming, can be instrumental in maintaining good physical and psychological health. Defining health as "a condition of adaptive responsiveness to the challenges of life," they assure us that dreaming can help us to constantly adapt by resolving life's ceaseless challenges in ways that do no disrupt the integrity and wholeness of the individual.[10] A classic example of this can be seen in the way the dreaming mind reacts to the vision of a monster or intruder. Drawing on Jung's theories about the psychologized shadow that often haunts dreams, LaBerge and Rheingold are adamant that bad dreams about monsters or intruders, especially those that recur, are actually messengers from our deep consciousness desperately trying to get our attention and tell us that there is some aspect of our psychological or physical makeup that needs help. If instead of continuing to try to outrun and evade these dream specters, we face them and ask them what they are trying to tell us, they will. In effect, heeding the message of the dream intruder prompts us to take a closer look at problems or issues we have been repressing, which, given the proper thought and attention, can lead to greater self-understanding and deep psychological and emotional healing.

DREAMING AS A MEANS OF SPIRITUAL HEALING

Healing dreams are necessarily psychosomatic in that the physical and psychological aspects of the dream body are organically connected to one another. Just as psychological problems can manifest themselves as physical ailments and vice versa, dreams that heal emotional agony also intrinsically heal physical pain. Another integral aspect of the dreaming self, the spirit, is often slighted, if not altogether neglected within the Western scientific approach to dream healing.

Psychologist Rubin R. Naiman claims that the sacred nature of dreaming is a product of the natural process of sleep as related to the sacred rhythm of night and day. He believes this rhythm has been compromised by the use of artificial light and demanding lifestyles that suggest we should be able to automatically fall asleep and wake up at times that suit our waking life demands and ignore the importance of our sleep and dream lives. Naiman says this disruption has created a culture that depends on unhealthy habits, such as using drugs and alcohol to induce sleep and caffeine to wake us back up, and that jeopardizes the sacred nature of sleep and dreams. "Night is home to a delicate spirituality," Naiman claims.

> There is a lovely, sacred, and mythic dimension to our night consciousness. Our challenge is to appreciate the mechanisms of sleep, dreams, and awakening without sacrificing their essential spiritual qualities.[11]

The incredible success of the Asclepian healing dream temples that lasted at least from 1300 BCE to 600 CE is no doubt due to the fact that they were ritually organized to heal not only the body and mind, but the soul as well. In his book *The Practice of Dream Healing,* psychotherapist Edward Tick suggests that, for this very reason, the modern world would do well to revive the Asclepian model of dream healing and integrate it into contemporary medical practices. He argues that modern medicine regards the human body as a machine that must be maintained to keep it free from pain and physical suffering. In this respect, medical practice tries to control fate by minimizing damage to the body and defeating death. Tick explains why this approach is not as effective as the Asclepian philosophy of dream healing:

> Sacred medicine as modeled by the Asclepian tradition comes out of a very different mindset. It is rooted in a soul-based worldview in which human consciousness experienced itself as part of an all-encompassing cosmic order. There is no such thing as a mind/body split in sacred medicine. Mind and body are coequal, fully interdependent, and inner expressive. The body is not a machine, but rather is the living carrier and container of soul on its journey through the world. The body is the material text of the soul, the living matter on which soul inscribes its conditions and signs and symptoms. Spiritual concerns, emotions, hopes and plans—all the "mind stuff" —are essential rather than peripheral to sacred medicine, because these functions are expressive of the soul.[12]

In other words, because modern medicine does not see the soul as an integral part of a human being and the source of the essential human concept of "self," it cannot achieve healing in a manner that is natural, holistic, and lasting. When we dream with the intent of healing ourselves, knowing that we are starting the process from within the depths of our souls, we open ourselves to the possibility for complete healing.

Another reason the Asclepian dream healing model was so successful was that, within it, the dream healing process was guided by what was perceived to be the Divine. Whether Asclepius personally appeared in the dream or instead sent one of his associate gods or goddesses, the trauma that prompted the dreamer to seek healing was completely addressed by a sacred dream presence. Just as when you cocreate art with the Divine, the experience of healing when you feel accompanied by the One who originally created the self who seeks wholeness and healing feels different from other attempts to heal.

Once you become adept at the art of sacred dreaming, the sacred presence can usually be detected in healing dreams that otherwise seem mundane—such as dreams about the state of the body, mind, and soul that use the dream metaphor of living in a house or driving in a car. The dreamer may experience the Divine sitting next to the dreamer, as a pervasive presence, or speaking to the dreamer from the background. Or the Divine may only be detected with later dream rehearsal, journal writing, or interpretation. Still, someone dreaming from the soul will find the sacred presence in a healing dream, and the relationship will hasten and enlighten the healing process.

The shamanic dream teacher Robert Moss believes that dream healing is soul work that affects the physical and psychological aspects of a person as well. The key to understanding how his method of dream healing works is his distinction between the spirit and the soul as it relates to the individual dreamer. In his book *Dreaming the Soul Back Home* he explains:

Spirit is perfect. We can't lose it, though we can lose contact with it; we can even forget that, beyond the skin, we *are* spirit. Soul is a different matter. It's our vital essence, and it is in a body to have adventures and to grow. Spirit does not evolve, but soul surely does. Also, you can't expect soul to stay in one place. When we suffer trauma or bitter disappointment or violent shock, soul may leave the body to escape. This produces the phenomenon that psychologists call dissociation and shamans call soul loss.[13]

From this analysis, we can see that, for Moss, spirit is a sacred field of Ultimate Reality that permeates everything and everyone, while soul is a spiritual reality related to the body and mind of each individual person. What is interesting about his shamanic understanding of dream healing—that the soul is trying to realize itself within the field of spirit—is that the soul is not confined by the embodiment of the dreamer. Moss reminds us that in Greek, the word for "soul" is *psyche,* which also means "butterfly." The soul flits in and out of the body, and when we lose our connection with it or with parts of it, we lose energy, memory, identity, personal gifts and skills, and the abilities to feel deeply and to choose and act from the heart. In all, we become lost to our life's purpose.[14] We can learn, however, to reclaim through our dreams the parts of our souls that have wandered away from us.

Moss recognizes that what he sees as "soul loss" is regarded within the discipline of modern psychology as a state of physical or mental denial, which results from the depression we enter when we suffer loss, oppression, or physical or psychological trauma. As Freud and especially Jung claimed, because within dreams we can more easily access the areas of our consciousness where these repressed feelings are stored, by analyzing these dreams we can reclaim lost parts of ourselves and effect psychological and sometimes physical healing. The difference in Moss's method of dream healing is that he focuses on the health and wholeness of the soul, knowing that within the integrated human self, once the soul becomes whole, most, if not all, other psychological and physical ailments of the self are usually healed as well. Moss describes some of the types of dreams that commonly signify the soul's quest to reclaim a lost part of itself. Among them are dreams about animals, houses, and a younger self as a separate person.

In dreams, Moss says, animals convey the state of our own vital energy or situation in life. He also tells us that we do not have to look for them in dreams, because our animal spirits are always seeking us. In many indigenous traditions, people believe that everyone is born with a connection with a particular animal that forms part of a totem of ancestry. This connection is evident to many people whose souls experience a connection with the spirit of nature and who have a lifelong rapport with a certain animal. Moss claims that this connection might also be reflected in a person's body type, lifestyle, or manner of responding to challenges.

He suggests three ways of interpreting or tracking the presence of dream animals within sacred dreams to understand how they metaphorically present us with parts of our lost souls. We should research a dream animal's natural habits and characteristics, follow its trail through folklore and myth, and embody its energy in the way we move and eat and use our physical senses. Moss cites the examples of borrowing the keen vision of the hawk, the ears of a fox, or the olfactory sense of the wolf. Dream animals might also appear as stand-ins for the behavior of others, in which case they might give us insight into how to interact with those people.[15]

In all, dream animals can help us to restore our souls and the rest of ourselves to health if we are attentive to what they have to say. Moss explains:

> Forming a strong connection with a dream animal is already soul recovery, restoring vital energy and clarifying

the natural path of that energy. The dream animal may prove to be a power animal, and a guide and protector for other forms of soul recovery for ourselves and others.[16]

Like Garfield, Moss says house dreams are important messages about the state of our body but adds that they may well reflect the state of the soul or a place where we can reclaim parts of our soul that we have lost. When we dream about a home we used to live in, that might suggest part of our soul that was lost when we lived there is calling us back to reclaim it. The reasons parts of the soul become estranged vary. Perhaps we mourned the death of a loved one when we lived there, or maybe we suffered a loss in the form of a failed romantic relationship. I would add that such dreams might occur because we were in our best physical or emotional health in this place and that the most robust or spiritual part of our soul is longing for reintegration into our present self. These dreams are incredibly common, and Moss suggests that when you have a dream of this nature, you ask yourself the question, "Did I leave a part of myself behind when I left that old situation?"[17]

Often we dream of being in a home that seems familiar, though we may have never lived in a house like the one in the dream, or we may find ourselves in an unfamiliar part of a house that is otherwise familiar. Jung's series of dreams in which he discovered his vocation as a depth psychologist were of this nature. He explained that, in the initial dream, he found himself descending the stairs of a house he described as strange but normal. When he ventured into the cellar, he entered a vault in the floor and found himself in a primordial cave with human remains and other archeological fragments. Here he developed his theory of the collective unconscious that humans have access to, especially in dreams, as well as the archaic remnants that he believed wait for all of us in the dark corners of the human consciousness.

You should note the details of your dream houses in your journal, whether they seem familiar or not, for sometimes the part of your soul energy that is waiting to be discovered there has been left or repressed by the consciousness for a reason. Because of this, it may be so shrouded in metaphor that its meaning may not be readily evident within the dream itself or even in later interpretation. But these houses often hold the essence of ourselves that we most desperately need to reclaim, so extra work and patience in exploring these dreams can be well rewarded with healing insights.

For example, I had written in my journal about several house dreams I never considered connected until one day when I read through the journal entries in one sitting. I was amazed to realize that though in each dream I was in a different house—none of which I had ever been in in my waking life—the floor plan of each was like the home I had grown up in. Then I noticed that in each dream I had stopped at a table that had a bright light suspended over it in such a way that it cast a deep, looming shadow of my head over the surface of the table. When I continued my symbolic analysis in light of the patterns that were emerging from this sequence of dreams, I learned a sacred lesson about my concept of myself in relation to my work, which had been suffering because, decades before, I had lost part of my essential soul-self while dealing with some of the traumatic demands of puberty. Realizing this helped me to reclaim her, along with a good measure of youthful hope, courage, and self-assurance.

Another fascinating manner in which the estranged parts of our souls often call to us in dreams is through characters that appear in dreams as manifestations of our younger selves. Moss says when you dream of yourself with a younger companion of the same sex, though you might initially think of the younger person as your child, grandchild, or sibling, ask yourself if the companion could be a manifestation of your younger self. As a frequent dreamer of younger soul-selves, I have found that the younger self may be male or female, and each manifestation may reveal powerful messages about where I am now psychologically and spiritually in relation to different phases in my psychological and spiritual development throughout my life.

I have also come to realize that dreams about very young children or infants for which the dreamer feels a strong emotional attachment often signify a longing for, or reclamation of, the pure, unadulterated sense of self that was probably experienced in early childhood but has dissipated throughout the years. These dream babies, as I like to call them, can carry especially strong spiritual healing messages, because they can remember the real soul essence of our selves that many of us have forgotten throughout years of trying to please everyone but ourselves and to answer a wide variety of social demands and moral expectations. These sacred dreams should be interpreted with care. Other unexpected dream visitors of any age, shape, or species may also manifest aspects of ourselves or the state of our soul-selves that we need to pay better attention to for the sake of physical, psychological, or spiritual healing.

THE ART OF SPIRITUAL-PSYCHOSOMATIC DREAMING

Using my own experience with sacred dreaming as a means of healing, coupled with the experiences of dreamers who have shared their sacred healing dream work with me, I would like to add a few observations to those of the dream healing experts mentioned above. In revisiting dreams that take place in a house or building, I have found that individuals who are spiritual, and especially those who have been working with a growing awareness of their own sacred dream spirals, not only usually experience the structures they are in within these dreams as the boundaries of their ensouled bodies, but often also have an awareness of it being placed within the sacred cosmos according to their religious or spiritual traditions or beliefs. Those who were raised with the Western religious understanding of the three-story universe, consisting of the earth beneath heaven and above hell, will often unconsciously superimpose this structure on the building in which they dream themselves. Consequently, ascending stairs in this dream can not only signify the condition of the spine, but can also represent rising to a higher sense of self and ultimately to heaven. Conversely, dreams of descending a staircase can signify descent into the aspects of the self that are felt to be in some way lower or even to some extent hellish or normally off-limits for one reason or another.

For dreamers with a strong spiritual consciousness, dreams in which they are confined within houses, buildings, or vehicles may indicate an awareness that their own soul or spirit is confined within their bodies. The placement of openings, windows, or doors within these dreams can signify opportunities for the soul to transcend the physical limitations of the body and revel in the freedom and totality of Spirit in the sense of total union with the Divine or Ultimate Reality.

Another dreamscape I have noticed that is often associated with the state of the body and soul of the dreamer is a sense of self superimposed on the natural landscape that aligns with the seven energy centers in the body. This naturescape of self corresponds to the seven chakras used for kundalini and tantric meditation in the South Asian traditions and also aligns with the ten *sefirot* as they are configured in the seven levels that comprise the Jewish Kabbalistic Tree of Life, which makes up the mystical body of God. From my experience, whether a person has any knowledge of chakra meditation or the Kabbalah, the energy that emanates from the seven body centers is sensed in the deep consciousness and avails itself metaphorically in dreams and mythology with a somewhat predictable pattern of symbols. In essence, humans seem to have an unconscious awareness of the sequence of their energy centers as they are aligned vertically from the ground up that tends to form an unconscious self-identity.

In my years of studying mythology and dreams, I have found that this sense of self as a continuum of energy that extends from the ground upward is also psychologically correlated to the sense of existing in a vertical spatial landscape that extends from the ground to the heavens—which is also made up of different levels of energy observable as a landscape made up of the natural elements. In all, we seem to have an archetypal understanding of the self as a microcosm of the universe. The natural landscape in which dreams take place can signal what energy center of the body is calling for attention within the dream. And because each energy center has its own encoded spiritual, psychological, and physical information about the inner workings of the self, working with these dreams as a sacred art can produce amazing healing of the body, mind, and soul.

Many successful methods of chakra meditation have been developed in different religious and cultural traditions. My method of understanding sacred energy center dreams draws on the Hindu method of kundalini, because it is the most ancient method extant. So the spiritual archaic remnants of the chakra energy system would have its roots in the Hindu kundalini tradition. The Hindu form of chakra awareness has also been historically recorded in art with a rich and complex system of symbols, integrating colors, shapes, and animals that are strikingly similar to the symbolic messages of myths and dreams. A thorough analysis of these is beyond the scope of this book, but an adept sacred dreamer would do well to keep an eye on these while researching cultural and archaic sources for dream symbols.

Important for the sake of sacred dream healing is the fact that, from the beginning of chakra practice, each energy center has been associated with particular sacred energy attributes that constitute the spiritual, social, mental, and physical aspects of the self. In applying chakra awareness as it appears within a dream landscape to contemporary methods of self-understanding and healing, I rely on the work of the spiritual healer Caroline Myss, who provided in her book *Anatomy of the Spirit* a remarkable explanation of the personal, social, and physical values associated with each of the chakras as they relate to the modern consciousness.

The energy center that forms the root of the human energy field is the *Muladhara* chakra, which is situated at the base of the spine. This is experienced as the field of incarnation, or spirit that has been born into flesh and bones, as well as the sense of groundedness or the physical reality of being human. The best way to physically locate this energy center in the body is to remember how this part of your body has seemed to seize when you have felt particularly afraid. Ancient sacred meditation on this chakra often included methods of strengthening it to dispel fear.

Dreams that take place within a setting that is noticeably grounded, underground, or in the bowels of the earth are often responding to the energies of this center in the body. Common dreamscapes that emanate from this sense of self include caves, canyons, burial or cremation grounds, dark jungles, and ocean floors. This energy center is also associated with the raw or animal nature of the human, so wild animals, such as venomous serpents, tigers, lions, and leopards, also abound in these dreams. This center has traditionally also been understood to govern the sense of smell, so dreams with a noticeable scent or odor might be associated with it.

Myss provides further valuable clues about how dreams of this nature can be interpreted as a means of healing, indicating that this energy center is also where our identity as part of a group is located. She associates it with the human need for tribal power and the identity and strength that comes from being part of a community. From this center arises our sense of justice, as well as the need for a spiritual foundation. Myss also asserts that the energy connection this center has with the physical body includes the spinal column, rectum, legs, bones, feet, and immune system. This is also the center of emotional and mental health. She goes on to say that primary fears associated with this chakra are those of physical survival, abandonment by the group, and loss of physical order. Its primary strengths include family identity, bonding, honor, and loyalty. Myss also distills what she calls a sacred truth from the energies of each chakra, which I find helpful in interpreting sacred dreams that take place in locations associated with them. For the first chakra, it is "All is one."[18]

The second energy center, the *Svadhisthana* chakra, is situated in the spine region above the genitals and below the waist. It is where you get that gut feeling about certain things. Tradition has it that this is the seat of the personality and controls the sense of taste. This is also the power center of initiative and creative energy and is strongly associated with reproductive sexual energy and birth or symbolic rebirth. In the world's mythology, the power of this energy is manifested in cycles of birth as associated with water—no doubt due to an unconscious sense of being in the womb and from observation of the natural birthing process, which is always presaged by a dramatic flow of water.

Dreams in which a body of water, such as an ocean, river, spring, or stream, is a predominant theme are often generated from the natural energies of the body centered here, especially those in which the dreamer has a sense of being submerged in water, floating on the surface of the water, or emerging from it. The first question you should consider about a dream like this is whether you feel you are being, or need to be, metaphorically rebirthed in some way.

Myss says that with this chakra the social energies shift from the sense of tribal relationship to those that satisfy more personal, physical needs. Emotionally and psychologically, it responds to the need for meaningful personal relationships and some control of the physical environment or perhaps even your financial situation. Fears associated with it include loss of control of the self because of addiction, rape, betrayal, impotence, financial loss, or abandonment. Its energy strengths are the ability and stamina to survive physically and financially on your own, the ability to take risks, resilience to recover from loss, the power to rebel, and the power to make decisions as part of self-re-creation. Its energy relates to the sexual organs, the womb, the large intestine, the lower vertebrae, pelvis, hip area, appendix, and bladder. Myss's sacred truth for this chakra is "Honor one another."[19]

The third center of human energy, the *Manipura* chakra, is located at the solar plexus. Sanskrit writings say this is the center of the balance for the energies of the individual and the apex of the life force with which the soul is connected to the cosmos. It guides the sense of sight and light, and its vital element is fire. I find that dreams related to this center of energy usually take place on land at the edge of a body of water. Interestingly, these dreams also often include a bonfire, campfire, or flame that many sacred dreamers sense represents their souls.

In light of this, we can understand why Myss says this is the chakra of personal power as it relates to the external world that mediates between external and internal consciousness. Dreams of this nature could indicate the need to pay attention to the body's physical needs concerning the stomach, pancreas, adrenals, upper intestines, gallbladder, liver, and the middle spine. Psychological and emotional needs expressed from this energy center relate to self-responsibility, self-esteem, fear of rejection, and oversensitivity to criticism. Strengths derived from it include self-esteem, self-respect, self-discipline, ambitions, the ability to handle crisis, the courage to take risks, generosity, ethics, and strength of character. Myss adds that the sacred truth of the third chakra is "Honor thyself."[20]

The fourth center of energy is located at the region of the spine closest to the heart. Accordingly, the *Anahata* chakra is the center of love and compassion. It is associated with the element of air and governs the human sense of touch. Dreams generated from this area often take place in areas of lush, fertile vegetation, including meadows, rolling green hills, flower gardens, and forests. Myss says that this chakra mediates between the body and spirit and determines their health and strength. It reflects our emotional perceptions and hence the quality of our lives.

Its energy connection to the body concerns the heart and circulatory system, the ribs, breasts, thymus gland, lungs, shoulders, arms, hands, and diaphragm. The fears that it deals with include fear of loneliness and commitment, the inability to protect oneself emotionally, and emotional weakness and betrayal. Loss of energy in the heart chakra can result in feelings of jealousy, bitterness, anger, hatred, and an inability to forgive others as well as oneself. The primary strengths of this energy center are love, forgiveness, compassion, dedication, inspiration, hope, trust, and the ability to heal oneself and others. The sacred truth Myss links with this chakra is "Love is divine power."[21]

The *Vishuddha* (meaning "pure") chakra is located at the throat where the spinal column and medulla oblongata (the lower half of the brainstem) are joined. It is the center of communication and healing. It is related to the element of ether and controls the principle of sound and the sense of hearing. For this reason, dreams with a strong audio component, such as a loud noise, noticeable music, or locutions may relate to the energy of this body center.

I have found that dreams related to the energy of this chakra often take place in environments that symbolize the juncture or liminal realm between the earth and the heavens. They can be set in the mountains and on or near bridges and may contain images of the horizon or rainbows. According to Myss, this chakra embodies the challenges of surrendering our own willpower and spirits to the will of God. It is involved in the power of choice, which Myss explains influences every detail of our lives and therefore every illness. It is connected to the energy of the throat, thyroid, trachea, esophagus, parathyroid, hypothalamus, neck, vertebrae, mouth, jaw, and teeth. Dreams generated from this energy center might involve fears of having no authority or power of choice within our lives, including fear of the will of the Divine. The strengths that can be derived from this chakra include faith, self-knowledge, and personal authority. The sacred truth Myss attributes to it is "Surrender personal will to divine will."[22]

The sixth energy center, the *Ajña,* is located in the head between the eyebrows. It is the wisdom center or "third eye" of the self and is in command of all the cognitive faculties of the mind. It processes mental images, abstract ideas, reasoning, and psychological skills. Dreams that manifest the health or wellness of this center often take place in the sky. Flying dreams—whether you are in a vehicle or airborne of your own power—can be speaking to interests of the wisdom center, as can dreams in which you are floating in the air or standing at the top of a tall tower, mountain, or any high vantage point, looking down at or to some extent aware of the earth far below. For example, a dream about a meeting on the top floor of a tall building that has an aerial view of the city below can signify aspects of the mind deliberating about a problem that the dreamer has been grappling with consciously or unconsciously. Attention to the proceedings may well lead the dreamer to a solution.

Myss adds that fears that may come out of this energy center include an unwillingness to look within and excavate your fears—fear of truth when your reasoning is clouded; fear of sound, realistic judgment, or discipline; and fear of your shadow self and its attributes. Strengths she associates with it are intellectual abilities, the capacity to evaluate your conscious and unconscious insights, receiving inspiration, intuitive reasoning, and emotional intelligence. The sacred truth she assigns to it is "Seek only the truth."[23]

The seventh chakra, the *Sahasrara,* is located outside the physical body about one handbreadth above the crown of the head. This is the energy center for union of the self with the spiritual world or the Divine. I believe it is universally felt, unconsciously if not consciously. Consider that in every cultural tradition, sacred figures are usually depicted with a halo surrounding their head, religious leaders often wear hats or headpieces that extend to this area, and political leaders often wear crowns with jewels that embellish the field of the crown chakra with reflecting light. It is symbolized in kundalini diagrams and literature by a thousand-petaled lotus inverted over the head as it showers the body with cosmic radiations. According to the kundalini expert Ajit Mookerjee, this chakra "synchronizes all colours, encompasses all senses and all functions, and is all-pervading in its power." He also says that it is the "center of quintessential consciousness, where integration of all polarities is experienced, and the paradoxical act of transcendence is accomplished in passing beyond ever-changing samsara and emerging from time and space."[24]

Dreams of ecstatic union with the Divine, either with a sense of the grandeur of the cosmos, or a conceptualization of heaven, are probably generated from this energy center. As it relates to the health of the dreamer, Myss says this chakra influences the major body systems, including the central nervous system, the muscular system, and the skin. She also says that it contains the energy that produces devotion, inspirational and prophetic thoughts, transcendent ideas, and mystical connections. She adds that it is the energy center for spiritual insight, vision, and intuition far beyond ordinary human consciousness. Fears regarding this center are related to spiritual issues, such as the dark night of the soul, and its strengths reflect all that is inherent in faith in the Divine, such as inner guidance, insight into healing, and trust that eclipses ordinary human fears. Its sacred truth is "Live in the present moment."[25]

Though dreams that take place in dreamscapes like these may not necessarily relate to the location of the human energy centers, they can alert us to parts of ourselves and our souls that might be in need of healing. Sacred dreams such as these may shed light on aspects of our physical, mental, emotional, and spiritual selves that might need medical attention, a change of lifestyle or personal habits, changes in attitude about someone or something, or a redirection of spiritual thought and energy. They may also help us to solve problems that often lead to mental, physical, and spiritual distress, or even depression. What is most exciting about the correlation between the energy centers in the body and the environment in which we live is that thousands of years of cultural and religious testimony bears up the reality that there is a highly charged spiritual relationship between the divinely designed cosmos and the soulscape of each individual that is especially conducive to sacred dream exploration.

Sacred Dreamself Mapping

I have adapted this method of dream healing from a practice of dream body mapping designed by Daniel Deslauriers that I learned in a seminar I took during my doctoral studies. The practice is deeply meditational. In the seminar, Deslauriers had recorded audio directions to guide the dreamer throughout the process, which was very effective. Because I cannot replicate that experience here, I suggest you familiarize yourself with steps 1 through 3 before you begin, and then try to work through the entire process from memory to avoid having to disrupt the meditative quality of your work. Wait to read the fourth and fifth steps until after you have created your dreamself map. If you do this, you will avoid unconsciously drawing based on the interpretive steps, and your map will more accurately convey the condition of your dreamself.

1. Draw a contour outline of your physical body.

Make this drawing life-size if possible. If you can, enlist the help of a friend to draw around the outline of your actual body. A smaller replica will suffice, but because mapping can require a lot of space and detail, make it as large as you feasibly can, and leave some blank space around the contour. Have coloring or drawing materials handy. I suggest using soft colored pencils or pastels, because they come in a wide range of colors, can be used without preparation, mixing, or blending, and can convey hard lines or soft-blurred edges—all of which may be extremely helpful in conveying the details of dream imagery. Select a dream that you felt contained a sacred healing message, and read your journal entry about it. If you have not written about it in your journal, spend some time free writing about it.

2. Meditatively visualize yourself within your sacred dream.

Reenter the mystical realm of dream consciousness through meditative breathing. Use the same general technique that you use for cultivating sacred dreams and creating sacred art. Sit in a comfortable position with your spine fully extended, or lie in the posture in which you usually sleep. Take a deep, comfortable breath and feel it filling your whole self. Hold the breath momentarily before exhaling slowly. Repeat breathing in this manner as you meditatively reenter your dream. As you breathe, be mindful of how your breath feels as each part of your being fills and deflates. Note any areas where your energy seems especially dynamic or blocked. Keep breathing until you can physically, mentally, emotionally, and spiritually feel how you felt within the dream. Your feelings may have changed or evolved within the dream. That is fine. Concentrate on your feelings of self as they flow throughout the dream.

3. Map your dreamself.

When you have recaptured the feeling of yourself as you were within the dream, spontaneously draw these feelings onto the map of your body contour in the same way you created your initial dream art. Let the colors choose you, and allow yourself to create your dream image as you remember how your dream body felt. If it changed throughout your dream, draw the later senses of your dreamself right over any earlier ones.

4. Use your dreamself map to understand the dream's sacred healing message.

When you look over your dreamself map after your meditation, you will probably be astounded to see how different parts of your body are holding your concerns and worries as well as your joys and triumphs. Thousands of messages about the state of your physical, psychological, and spiritual health may manifest themselves in thousands of different ways. Follow your instincts in interpreting your map, just as you would in interpreting your sacred dreams. Within your analysis, however, I suggest you ask yourself these questions:

- What parts of yourself seem tight or congested, and what parts seem open and free to function normally?

- Where does your energy reside, and from where does it seem to radiate? Does it extend beyond the confines of your embodiment?

- Where is your soul in your map? Is in intact, scattered, or missing altogether?

- Where is the sacred presence in this map?

- How does your map relate to other symbols in the dream once they are amplified?

Write your answers to these questions and all your other thoughts and discoveries about your sacred dreamself map in your sacred dream journal.

5. Honor your dreamself by attending to its needs.

If your sacred dreamself mapping indicates there might be a physical or psychological problem, seek the proper medical or psychiatric care. If it indicates you are too stressed or overworked, find a way to relax. If tension or dynamism seems localized on or near one of the body's natural chakra energy centers, check to see if any of the symptoms, fears, or strengths above seem to apply. Aided with this knowledge, you might find that regular meditation on scenes from dreams that were located within certain energy centers can work wonders. If the dream imagery was troubled, meditate on the same setting while creating a calmer, more satisfying dream sequence. Use this imagery as an intention with which to cultivate future healing dreams. Above all, trust your instincts in interpreting your dreamself image, and trust that your sacred dreams are perennially trying to heal you.

CHAPTER NINE

THE NUANCES OF GENDER IN SACRED DREAMING

The levels of dreaming consciousness relate to the dreamer's personal experiences, embodiment, and a variety of cultural influences, as we have seen. Obviously, the society within which we live has a tremendous effect not only on our waking lives, but on our dreams as well. Anthropologist Erika Bourguignon has shown how dreaming plays a crucial role in an individual's ability to deal with interpersonal relationships and situations.[1] The primary and most easily observable difference between human beings within any society is that we are divided into two distinct types—male and female. Of course, we can see that this difference is necessary to perpetuate the survival of our species. But it also brings with it a host of other wonderful yet complicated interpersonal relationships that must be dealt with on one level of consciousness or another. Because of this, one of the most prevalent factors affecting social and cultural dream content is that of gender—or the gender identity of the dreamer.

Neuropsychologist John Boghosian Arden explored the sociocultural dynamics of dreams in his book *Consciousness,*

Dreams, and Self and discovered that a strong relationship between your gender and the general character of your dream content can be seen across cultures and socioeconomic groups. Moreover, as your position and experience within the group changes, so does your dream content. From his research, he concludes that there is a direct relationship between gender, dream content, and culture.[2] He illustrates how this association has progressed in modern times by comparing studies of gendered dream content that have been done over a period of thirty years.

He begins with the findings of an extensive study done by the Dream Research Institute in 1966 involving some 30,000 dreams of people from all over the world. In this investigation, some of the gender differences that manifested themselves were that men appeared in men's dreams twice as often as women did, while women tended to dream equally about men and women and reported friendlier encounters with the men in their dreams. Women dreamt more about being indoors and in familiar settings, with more people—usually people they knew. Men had much more aggression in their dreams, often physical violence that was usually directed toward unfamiliar males. When women did dream of aggression, it was usually more verbal. Men's dreams tended to involve more physical activity and adventure, and women's dreams tended to be more emotional. In addition, women reported that they dreamt in color more often than men.[3]

In comparing the findings of the Dream Research Institute with similar studies done thirty years later—after a strong sociocultural shift toward more equality for women—he saw less differentiation in male and female social interaction, misfortune, and aggression, but men still tended to dream of more strangers and male characters, and women's dreams still contained more emotional content, family members, babies, and indoor settings.[4] In all, he concluded, the basic differences in men's and women's dreams are due not only to their differences in embodiment, but also to the way their embodiment or gender identity is constantly being shaped and reshaped by their social and cultural relationships.

This phenomenon is particularly apparent when examining social and cultural effects on sacred dreaming recorded in the texts of the world's religions. A close look at social and gender influences on mystical dreaming has astounding ramifications not only for understanding how the world has evolved culturally, but for the way we as contemporary sacred dreamers contribute to world culture.

GENDER WITHIN THE CONTEXT OF SACRED DREAM HISTORY

A full appreciation of the nuances of gender within sacred dreaming requires recognition that most of the recorded scriptures of the world were written by men for a male readership, with the assumption that the agents and beneficiaries of their social and religious cultures were also primarily male. In light of this, from the perspective of sacred dream history, any female dream activity was designated as such; therefore, any mention of women dreamers or women's roles in sacred dreaming reflects the patriarchal society's attitude about the importance of gender in dreaming. For this reason, the gender implications of sacred dreaming in most cases reflect women's roles as they are valued by men. This is unfortunate when we consider that in Bulkeley's study on mystical dreams, he discovered not only that about half of the population has mystical dreams, but also that they are experienced by many more women than men.[5]

In the ancient Eastern traditions, gender became a matter of importance in dreams insofar as dreams were closely related to creation. The Hindu Vedas were largely written several centuries BCE, after the Aryan culture entered the Indus Valley region of northwestern India. One of the aims of the Aryan Brahman priests who wrote the texts was to supplant the worship of the indigenous goddess figures responsible for fertility, crop growth, and the cycles of nature[6] with a patriarchal religion guided by an exclusively male priesthood. As a result, the *Sama Veda* has it that the world was created from the navel of the sleeping god Vishnu as he slept on the coils of a giant snake in the midst of a vast ocean.

Another Vedic reference to sacred dream sleep contains a prayer to Agni, the fire god, to protect women from demons who might take sexual advantage of them in the night or harm pregnant women and their fetuses. Bulkeley notes that "what mattered to the Brahmans was maintaining the proper order of human-Divine relationships. Discouraging women's sexual dreaming was a small but necessary part of the process."[7] Consequently, the association between dreams and childbirth became the prevailing reason why women were mentioned in Eastern religious scripture. To that end, the conception of major male religious figures, including the Jain Mahavira and the Buddhist Siddhartha Gautama Buddha, occurred within their mother's dreams. Conversely, in scriptures as well as the medical texts of ancient India, when a woman appears in dreams (usually the goddess Durga or Kali in Hinduism or Mrtyu in early Buddhist texts), the appearance is a prophecy of illness or even death, especially if she is disheveled in appearance, has dark skin, wears red clothing, or has red eyes.[8]

Ancient South Asian texts suggest anointing the dreamer's eyes with the milk from a young nursing girl's or goddess's breasts. As Buddhist scholar Serinity Young notes, this emphasizes the belief that dreams are "seen" and not "had" and that they are an external gift of prophecy from the Divine rather than a matter of internal psychological activity. Young also says that this gives us the sense that the "power of the dream" is such that "the dreamer not only sees the dream but can be seen by it."[9]

As mentioned in the earlier investigation of historical dream interpretation, in ancient China peasant women who were believed to be adept at spirit communication were employed by Chinese emperors as dream interpreters. Traditional Buddhist texts also offer accounts of women's prophetic dream capabilities, including one in which Siddhartha's wife, Gopa, predicted that he would desert her and their infant son for a life of asceticism. When she related the dream to Siddhartha upon awakening, he allayed her fears by rejecting the prophecy of the dream, even though it turned out to be true.

Traditional and contemporary Tibetan Buddhist dream techniques emphasize ritual visualization of female deities and *dakinis*—translated "sky-goers." A dakini is a female intermediate spiritual being who can bestow powers that lead to enlightenment, guard dreamers from any intruder who might seek to harm them in their sleep, and dispel any karmic traces that might result in bad dreams.

In Egyptian historical dream incubation, the goddesses Hathor and Isis were often invoked. The Ramesside *Dream Book* contains a ritual spell to ward off nightmares in the form of a dialogue between Isis, the regenerative mother goddess of healing, and her son Horus, who had been suffering from nightmares. "Do not divulge that which you saw," Isis warns him, "in order that your numbness may be completed, your dreams retire, and fire go forth against that which terrifies you."[10]

Bulkeley writes:

Everywhere we look in classic Greek culture—in drama, poetry, history, and medicine—we find dreaming represented as both a valuable source of heavenly knowledge and as a frightening portal into the nether regions of the psyche and the cosmos.[11]

Female dreamers and dream goddesses were often the means by which both were communicated. Homer's *Odyssey* portrays the force of a woman's sacred prophetic dream wherein the goddess Athena came to her and assured her that her son, Telemachus, was protected by the gods and would come home safely. Another example of this is Sophocles's play *Hecuba*, in which the heroine has a harrowing nightmare about the death of her children that had been sent from the goddess Earth, the womb of dreams. In this respect, the mythology that formed the basis of dreams was founded on the belief that they "were born of the primordial female power of the earth, the goddess Chthon, whose oracle at Delphi was stolen from her by Apollo. In retaliation, she created dreams."[12]

As also noted earlier, particularly in the instance of the goddesses who interpreted Gilgamesh's dreams in Mesopotamia, though kings were usually the recipients of sacred dreams, a goddess or female relative almost always interpreted its meaning. Sacred dreams were valued as potent vehicles of prophecy throughout the Hebrew Scriptures; however, though the Book of Joel affirms that sons and daughters will prophesy (2:28) and strong female prophets do arise in these texts, spiritual dreaming and dream interpretation seem to remain exclusively male prerogatives.

In the Christian Scriptures, Mary conceives Jesus by the power of the Holy Spirit through the visitation of an angel, but in contrast to similar dreams of conception in the Eastern traditions, Joseph receives the actual conception dream (Matt. 20:23) as well as three other prophetic dreams including information on what to name the child and how to protect him from Herod. When Jesus is brought before Pontius Pilate for questioning, Pilate's wife sends her husband the message not to condemn him, for she had had a troubling yet prophetic dream that he was a righteous man (Matt. 27:19). Paul wrote in his epistles of four prophetic dreams that had the same character as the ancient Middle Eastern sacred dreams—that is, a sacred presence stood over him as he slept and imparted divine wisdom.

Despite the early Christian mistrust of dreams, in the first century CE the Shepherd of Hermas recorded the details of a dream vision in which the early church as it was forming took on the persona of a goddess who had descended from heaven to admonish him for his sins on behalf of the God who is "the creator of beings out of nothing." Bulkeley makes the brilliant observation that the Shepherd of Hermas's dream, like those of Joseph and Paul, served as a sort of "psychospiritual trans-formation" for members of the fledgling faith who needed not just a change of behavior, but a change of heart in order to withstand the coming centuries of Christian persecution.[13] In short, dreams helped the members of the fledgling religion to create an identity that would sustain them mentally and physi-cally throughout the course of Christian history. Perhaps the most poignant example of how sacred dreams helped bring about this transformation was recorded in the Passion account of Vibia Perpetua of Carthage. Not only was she able to incu-bate prophetic dreams before her violent execution in the arena, but the content of her dreams in association with her social sta-tus as a nursing mother were foundational in establishing early Christian sacramental theology—especially regarding the role of the church as a mother who nurses her children through Baptism and the Eucharist.[14]

In the Qur'an, several suras attest to the fact that Muhammad believed his dreams revealed the will of Allah. The seventeenth sura, "The Night Journey," was a visionary experience in which he was transported to heaven and taught the ethical, legal, and moral principles that would become the foundation of the Muslim faith.[15] The sura does not specifically say that this vision was a dream, but Bulkeley notes:

> The visionary quality of the experience and its allusion to an airborne journey to otherworldly realms, combined with the fact that it happened at night, supports the belief that it was a dream.[16]

In the fifty-seventh sura, "The Star," Allah reminds Muhammad to consider the guidance of three particular female beings (53:19–27). One of Muhammad's earliest biographers wrote that this sura was written in response to the Meccan people who were reluctant to give up their belief in some of the traditional Persian deities as they embraced Islam. In response to this, Muhammad had a vision in which God said to him, "Have you considered al-Lat and al-Uzza and Manat, the third, the other? These are exalted birds, whose intercession is approved." Bulkeley explains:

> The three goddesses, known together as "the daughters of Allah" had long been worshiped at special temples in Mecca and other cities around Arabia. When Muhammad recited these verses, the recitation was enthusiastically welcomed by the Meccans as a sign that he was acknowledging a harmonious continuity between his new religious teachings and traditional Arabian worship practices. Allah was indeed the supreme creator, to be revered as such, and the goddesses al-Lat, al-Uzza, and Manat were acknowledged to be divine intermediaries between God and the human realm and thus deserving of devotion in their own right.

But then Muhammad had another nocturnal revelation, perhaps the most startling one yet. Gabriel spoke to him by night and severely chastised him for reciting words that came not from God but from Satan (*shaitan*). The earlier verses about the three goddesses must be removed from the *Qur'an*, Gabriel commanded, and new verses inserted in their place. These new verses (sura 53:23) categorically rejected the goddesses as legitimate deities worthy of any attention, dismissing them as mere projections of human fantasy.[17]

In her essay "Women and Dream Interpretation in Contemporary Iran," dream scholar Parisa Rahimian relates that the art of dream interpretation is an integral aspect of Iranian cultural identity, which "acts as a common thread in expressing the feminine side of the culture as a whole."[18] She notes that most popular monthly magazines targeted at female audiences carry a regular section on methods of dream interpretation. She also asserts that dreaming has long been a source of indirect power and authority for women in Iran, citing the example that

> when an important family decision needs to be made, the husband is usually the final authority, but the wife's voice is more apt to be included if she describes a dream relating to the matter at hand.[19]

Rahimian relates that the art of dream interpretation is passed between women from one generation to the next and usually involves referencing dream dictionaries in conjunction with intuition and oral traditions as well. Based on her examination of the common dream dictionaries that were used in comparison to the regional ritual lore, she also shares her astonishing insight that dreaming forms a feminine bridge between pre-Islamic and Islamic traditions. She states:

What I found especially interesting was that most of the dream dictionaries attributed their teachings to Islamic sources, while orally transmitted practices either had nothing to do with Islam or were a mixture of Islamic and pre-Islamic traditions. I could find numerous traces of pre-Islamic goddess cults in these practices, residing uneasily in the dominant Islamic paradigm. For example, some women say that if you have a negative dream, you should not tell the dream to anyone, but instead tell the dream to a water stream such as a river or (in the modern cities) to running water from the faucet. This principle of not sharing your bad dream with others can also be found in Islamic dream traditions, but telling the dream to a stream of water is not part of that tradition to my knowledge. Yet one of the greatest goddesses worshiped in ancient Persia was Anahita, who was the protector of water. The association with Anahita and water is so strong that sometimes she is specifically called the goddess of water. In this example we can see how dreaming has played a subtle role as a bridge between pre-Islamic and Islamic cultures, although such a connection might not be obvious at first glance.[20]

In many of today's religious shamanic or indigenous traditions, the power and wisdom of women's as well as men's dreams are often held in high regard. In his essay "Sending a Voice, Seeking a Place: Visionary Traditions among Native Women of the Plains," Lee Irwin, chair of the department of religious studies at Charleston College and author of books on Native American Spirituality, notices that among the shamans of the Native American Plains, men usually sought portentous dreams in a structured vision quest, but for women it was more often a "spontaneous arising," either in sleep or waking life—an intense, vivid, visionary dream without the dreamer necessarily making any attempt to see such a vision. He quotes his Lakota grandmother, a respected holy woman named Blue Earring:

> For women it is different from how it is for men. A woman's calling is in her dreams: it is usually powerful, spontaneous. She does not always need to be trained in the way that a holy man would.[21]

Irwin sums up his essay by saying that dreaming for women in these cultures is not so much a function of an active search as it is a discovery of deep potential.[22]

GENDER, SACRED DREAMS, AND THE EVOLUTION OF HUMAN HISTORY

Although most of these dream accounts were recorded by men for the edification of other men, much can be learned about the historical-cultural mind-set concerning gender in relation to the art of sacred dreaming by evaluating what these sacred texts say about women as artful sacred dreamers. Women's agency as sacred dreamers or dream interpreters has been valued most in (1) their conception dreams of male religious leaders, (2) their prophetic or shamanic dreaming wisdom, and (3) instances in which women have played important roles within men's ritualized sacred dreaming—including as spiritual guides and dream interpreters.

On the rare occasions when women appear as active agents of their own dreams, the most prevalent type of dream experienced by a woman according to the scrolls of the world's major religions is the "conception dream," in which she dreams of a divine source impregnating her with a male child of great spiritual importance. Young notes that conception dreams are fairly common in the stories of heroes and religious figures all around the world, including not only those of Jesus, Siddhartha Buddha, Krishna, and Lao Tzu, but also the Macedonian conqueror Alexander, and the Persian prophet Zoroaster. She remarks that these dreams have traditionally served as a "form of passive conception that represented women as incubators for predominantly male heroes."[23] I would add that this is a deep-conscious dream construct of cultures that are establishing a male creator godhead over and against cultures that were centered on the numinous creative powers of the ancient regenerative goddess religions that had prevailed for millennia in the same regions.

We should remember that while today most of us are taught that the history of civilization and religion began in the Western world with the Hebrew patriarchs and in the East with the arrival of the Aryans in the Indus Valley, what has generally been regarded as "prehistory" consists of thousands of years of largely matriarchal agricultural communities whose dominant deity was the great goddess of creation and regeneration. As historian Gerda Lerner reminds us, even after the patriarchal religions took root, the transference from goddess religious cultures to patriarchal-god religious cultures was far from immediate. In fact, it happened over a period of 2,500 years.[24] During this time, a hybridization of god-goddess religions was developing in the various cultures. While the act of creation is increasingly understood as an exclusively male-god enterprise, the numinous act of giving human birth—even to an auspicious male religious figure—still can be done only by a female. The dream, therefore, becomes the vehicle through which the male godhead creates the ability to give birth to sacred progeny through the body of the human female.

The historical sacred dream accounts concerning women's nursing—for example, about the Christian female martyr Perpetua—could be seen as a continuation of this pattern. In her prison diary, as her infant son no longer needed to nurse and her lactation ceased, she dreamt she ascended to heaven and was given milk from a God-like figure as he extracted it from a goat. Here caring for the infant creatures of the world becomes a divine male prerogative through the vehicle of the sacred dream. We also have the example of the South Asian practice of applying a young nursing girl's or goddess's milk to one's eyelids as a form of dream incubation. In this case, because a woman's lactation is the preferred ointment of sacred dream sight, the goddesses' life-giving and sustaining powers as they are related to dreams were at least subliminally still valued.

Curiously, the prophetic power of women's dreams was held in particularly high regard within the Western religious traditions where women's sacred dreams were downplayed in scripture and dreaming in general was often regarded with suspicion. In ancient Greece, Athena entered Penelope's dream to predict the safe return of her son, and the goddess Chthon gave birth to dreams through her oracle at Delphi, where women ritually foretold the future. Pilate's wife's dream warned against the injustice of executing Jesus, and though Pilate did not exonerate him, he had enough respect for her abilities as a prophetic dreamer to make sure he did not personally issue the death sentence. Rahimian tells us that in contemporary Iranian culture, women's dreams are often heeded by the men in their lives, even when their open thoughts and opinions are not, and the potency of a female shaman's prophetic dreams have never been doubted in indigenous traditions.

In both Eastern and Western traditions, the appearance of dark goddesses in dreams is also feared as portent of illness or death. We have seen this in the case of Durga or Kali in Hinduism, Mrtyu in Buddhism, and Chthon in Greece. These are, however, only a few examples of the many dark, female, womb-to-tomb figures who symbolize the cosmic mother who "brought you into the world and can take you back out again" and are found in the sacred and mythological literature of the world. On the surface, the pervasive presence of the sacred dark mother of the dreamworld may seem odd, but when considered within the context of the transference of ancient goddess regenerative religions into patriarchal god-creator religions, we see that the dark goddess who calls us to our deaths is the missing link in the natural regenerative cycle of life. As her creative powers are slowly but surely co-opted, her looming presence as the degenerative force of life becomes more exaggerated on a deep-conscious level.

Though women's agency as sacred dreamers is largely repressed throughout religious history, aside from conception dreams and those in which they serve as psychopomps of doom, the history of sacred dream texts shows that female deities or intermediaries between the human and divine realms have appeared as authoritative, if not forceful, guides within men's mystical dreams. Here we are reminded of the goddesses who stood at the head of dreaming kings, Isis's guidance of Horus's dreams, and the goddess who reprimanded and redirected the Shepherd of Hermas's dreams of ecclesiastical theology. Referring to the example of the Tibetan Buddhist dakini guides and protectors of sacred dreams, Young comments, "The dakinis point to the well-known theme in world religion and mythology of male dependence on a female guide in order to complete quests, win a goal, or achieve enlightenment."[25]

The goddesses of Mesopotamia and the contemporary women of Iran attest to the broad historical reverence for women's natural ability to interpret sacred dreams. In all, there seems to be an undeniable universal appreciation for the ominous power of women's dream interpretation. This may have to do with the fact that the dark-mother archetype is also strongly associated with mystical wisdom because knowledge of the realities of death—the other side of life—is without doubt the most sought after form of wisdom in the world's religious texts. It may also have much to do with the observation of women's intuitive capabilities in dealing with situations that arise in their everyday lives and personal relationships.

The "his-story" of the bulk of the world's recorded scriptures was recorded in a patriarchal attempt to supplant the world's prehistory of matriarchal cultures in which the major deities were largely goddesses whose regenerative powers maintained the cyclical pattern of natural birth, growth, and death, and rebirth. Yet the goddess regenerative archetype kept rising through the patriarchal religious dreams in the same way cultural and psychological archetypes continue to enter personal dreams. Apparently, while the numinous mystery and divinely imbued gift of female motherhood could be repressed from consciousness, it could not be eradicated from the deep-conscious awareness of dreams.

GENDER, SACRED DREAMS, AND THE FUTURE OF HUMAN EVOLUTION

From this brief historical perspective on the nuances of gender in the context of religious scriptural dreaming, we see that Arden's theory that there is a direct relationship between gender, dream content, and culture holds true. In the case of sacred dreaming, we also see that not only does the gender of the individual dreamer or subject being dreamed about become a critical aspect of the meaning and impact of the dream, but the gender of what is perceived to be the divine or sacred presence in the dream does as well. The history of sacred dream and mystical activity has proven that the enculturated psychosocial gender identity of the dreamer in relation to the perceived gender of the Divine adds another complicated angle to the human-divine relationship.

Another important fact that can be discerned from this perspective is that, although we often dream of Ultimate Reality in the way we are religiously and socially enculturated to do so, most adept sacred dreamers are aware that other faces or spiritual presences of the Divine, most likely from deeper levels of spiritual consciousness, manifest themselves in their dreams as well. The gripping truth in all of this is that the human concept of the Divine has historically been formed within the realm of human dreams and will continue to evolve as humans refine the art of sacred dreaming.

On a purely conscious level, the need to anthropomorphize the Divine, or to assign to it human attributes such as the quality of being male or female, light or dark, old or young, obviously stems from a deep desire to develop a personal relationship with it. One of the unfortunate results of this phenomenon is that when a certain type of person is associated with the Divine, that type of person tends to be honored as more "god-like" than other types of people in the same society. This association often results in systems of "othering" that create biases concerning not only gender, but also race, age, and class in a manner that can be construed as divinely sanctioned.

In addition, because of the limitations of personal pronouns such as "he," "she," or "it," which designate gender in English and some other languages, most religious discussion and religious education about the Divine is gender-specific. However, theologically speaking, most contemporary religions affirm that Ultimate Reality is essentially neither male nor female, dark nor light, young nor old, large nor small—but purely spirit and beyond the limits of conscious understanding. The exciting thing about sacred dreaming is that we can enter states of consciousness where we can free ourselves of these mental limitations. With practice, you can perfect the art of experiencing the fullness of divinity without having to distort or reconstruct its essence.

The Art of Accessing the
Divine Essence in Dreams

1. Reevaluate the essence of the Divine as it has appeared in dreams you have had.

Go back through the entries in your sacred dream journal and make a list of instances in which you believe you had an experience of the Divine. Try to mentally and emotionally reenter these particular dreamscapes and remember how each encounter felt.

This is where keeping a journal with a detailed thick description of the sequence and symbolism in your sacred dreams really pays off, because the essence of the Divine Spirit is without human biological constraints and its presence is truly ineffable. Human words—spoken or written—will not do it justice. However, a detailed journal account will usually help you to reenter the sensual and emotional aspects of the dream. Once you feel you have reestablished the sensation of being in the presence of the Divine, impose the spiritual imprint of that feeling in your mind and heart.

The best way I can describe this, to the best of my abilities as a sacred dreamer and a writer, is by sharing my first and most startling dream sensation of being in the presence of the Divine. I dreamt I was descending a spiral staircase to the central floor of a building infused with natural light. A figure that was obviously the source of the light—a human shape that extended from the basement floor to an opening in the roof several stories above but was not distinguishable as either male or female—stood in the middle of the stairwell with its arms open in a gesture of acceptance. A dark human figure in a trench coat, also with indistinguishable features, was huddled at the bottom of the stairs, surreptitiously watching me as I took the last few steps. When I reached the landing, I realized I was on the ground floor. Without thinking, I walked through a double glass door into a foyer. As I stepped into the foyer, the dark figure whooshed through the doors behind me and entered my dream body. Together we seemed to fly through another double glass door and over the sidewalk of an incredibly beautiful garden. Both sets of doors stood open behind us. At once a flood of energy overcame us. (I was aware in the dream that the dark figure and I had been fused, but we still had distinct characters.) I was profoundly aware that the figure of light, still inside the building, was the Divine and the source of the energy. I found myself floating in an incredibly peaceful infusion of perfect well-being that seemed to last a long time. I distinctly remember thinking to myself within the dream that I knew I could enter this state any time I wanted to, but in waking life I was too afraid to do so.

I awoke from this dream with an overwhelming realization that something amazing had happened. Though I was lucid enough in the dream to know I was dreaming and had entered a state that I could not or would not enter in my waking consciousness, at this time I was unfortunately not a proficient enough lucid dreamer to try to engage the divine spiritual-energy light figure or the mysterious dark figure in conversation. With later dream work I came to discover that the dark figure was my repressed "other self," or, as Jung would call it, my psychologized shadow or animus. When it entered me, I became a whole person. When the Divine presence sent light and energy through the newly integrated me, I left my physical embodied sense of self and experienced what I understood to be my essential spiritual self.

What was most revealing to me about this dream was that my spiritual self was a trinitarian infusion of my conscious self, my repressed deep-conscious self, and without any doubt in my mind, the Divine, who had entered my dream from a level of consciousness I could not identify. The relationship was charged with positive energy that resulted in a feeling I could never adequately describe. I am convinced that this dream encounter was an out-of-body experience, and it was infinitely more wonderful than anything I had experienced before.

I was so awestruck and to some extent frightened by this dream that I did not write it down immediately. Fortunately, the dream was so forceful that it imprinted itself indelibly on my mind, so when I did write it down, I was able to do so with a great deal of detail. After revisiting it later, I know that the divine essence was not so much the figure of light that stood in the open stairwell—that was the image of the Divine I had been enculturated to "see," but it was that wonderful sensation of the flow of benevolent energy that moved through my new sense of self as a reunited relational entity.

I have found several other sacred dreamers who have had similar experiences of the divine essence within their sacred dreaming, but for many others the encounter is totally different from mine. It stands to reason that every sacred dreamer will have a unique experience of the Divine, just as every relationship is unique in character. The objective is to discover what that particular feeling is for your own relationship with the Divine and focus on that in continuing your sacred dream work.

2. Use your deep-dream conscious knowledge of the Divine to incubate new sacred dreams.

Once you identify the relationship feeling or sensation that you share with the Divine, analyze it, celebrate it in your sacred dream art, and use that feeling to incubate further sacred dreaming. I suggest also setting a dream intention to become lucid in your dreams, because the ability to communicate with the sacred presence can bring astounding results. As you do your presleep meditative breathing, instead of reciting a mantra, allow yourself to sink back into the dreamscape where you experienced your most profound sensation of being in the presence of Ultimate Reality. If you have not yet had such a dream experience, allow yourself to feel that you are in the presence of the Divine, trying not to visualize it in any particular way. Everyone I know who has had this experience explains that it is accompanied by an overwhelming sense of peace, calm, and goodness, so let these feelings surround you as well.

3. Allow your concept of and relationship with the Divine to naturally evolve throughout the spiral of your sacred dream process.

As your relationship with the Divine grows and matures within your dreams, carry all this new knowledge into your waking life and throughout the spiral of your sacred dream work. If you let your spirituality naturally evolve within the fullness of your relationship with the Divine, your more mature understanding of it will affect other people's ideas about Ultimate Reality as well. Even if you cannot put that new awareness into words, it will enter into the realm of world consciousness and contribute to the evolution of humanity's growing awareness of itself. Humankind's ever-growing and ever-changing concepts of creation, culture, and religion are continually formed and reformed by sacred dreams.

NURTURING THE SACRED IN DREAMS

Spirit is always at work in dreams. Only those who are open to its work from within the different levels of consciousness can fully accept all the wonderful gifts that their dreams have to give them. Deslauriers makes the connection between dream work and spiritual enrichment. He says that after many years of working with people and listening to their dreams, he began to see that the psychological work related to dreams is often linked to something deeply spiritual. This observation prompted him to infer that dream work leads to the development of spiritual and emotional intelligence. "When people work with dreams in a sustained manner over time," Deslauriers writes, "they develop certain skills that foster psychological and spiritual insight."[1] These skills include (1) improved metaphorical and imagistic thinking that can express spiritual concerns and open up dimensions of experience unavailable through more rational means; (2) increased appreciation of the nuances of dream life and different types of dreams, which can prompt the dreamer to reevaluate her assumptions about the nature of reality and expand the boundaries of self-understanding; (3) increased openness to the creative potential of the mind and development of an understanding of intentional dreaming, which cultivates self-awareness and the dynamics between the self and others as well as your creative role in your perception of the world; (4) better understanding of the fluid boundaries between the body and the mind; (5) increased ability to apply guidance from dreams, which often call for transformative action; and (6) increased empathy toward others.[2]

The potential for spiritual growth and personal fulfillment through the art of sacred dreaming is vast and exciting. We should also recognize at this point that sacred work within the dream spiral of incubation, navigation, recall, journal writing, interpretation, expressive art, and healing can take you in a number of different directions. As we have seen, work with just one dream symbol can evolve into a fascinating though lengthy and sometimes complicated process. In light of the countless ways in which your dream work might take you, be mindful not to "overwork" your sacred dream life.

Rely on your personal instincts as well as your growing awareness of the guidance you are receiving from the sacred presence that emerges within your dreams when deciding what aspects of your mystical dream life to pursue and which ones to let go of. You can assure yourself you will not be missing any crucial information because any concept of the deep-dream consciousness that really demands your attention will be presented to you over and over again, whether through one recurring dream or a recurring pattern of symbols within different dreams, until you get it. So if you miss working with an important sacred dream metaphor now, you will surely have an opportunity to do so later.

Thorough sacred dream work can be time-consuming. One particularly frustrating aspect of this work may be the fact that once you begin working with the different aspects of your mystical dream life, the experience becomes so enthralling that you are tempted to spend more time on it than your schedule will allow. This is one reason sacred dream retreats can be so wonderful. Taking a week off from the other demands of life to immerse yourself in sacred dream techniques with other like-minded dreamers can greatly accelerate your skills as a sacred dreamer. With adequate unhurried time and space to incubate dreams, sleep without interruption, write in a journal, and create related works of dream art, many people become avid sacred dreamers who had previously had difficulty kick-starting the process within their busy lives. The retreat setting is also a perfect place for sacred dream group work.

The value of group sacred dream work can be monumental. Indigenous communities have used group dream work for spiritual and therapeutic purposes throughout the history of humankind. Sharing dreams during the morning meal has long been a means of divination, prophecy, and retaining a spiritual bond with deceased ancestors. Bulkeley tells the story of how in mid-twentieth-century Egypt, when the Nile Valley was over-taken by the Muslim-Sufi religious culture, the Nubian people were able to preserve their community by sharing their dreams to help reestablish their physical and spiritual cultural roots.[3]

The amazing thing that happens when people meet regularly to share their sacred dreams is that the dream spiral expands to become a communal journey. Not only do many of the same dream symbols and metaphor patterns tend to occur within the dreams of more than one dreamer, but participants commonly report having shared identical dream stories or even having participated in the same dream.

Connie Cockrell Kaplan facilitates women's dream circles and advocates using an ancient method of structuring group dream work as a means of cultivating ceremony, power, and holy energy. She notes that after each dreamer tells her dream to the circle and every other member mirrors the dream back with her own insights, the members of the circle come to realize that their dreams are not individual but that they are all dreaming together, and their dreams "fit together like puzzle pieces."[4]

Moss has developed a method to guide dreamers in sharing the dreamscape while awake that he calls dream "tracking." First, a dreamer shares his dream as simply and clearly as possible, then a dream partner asks questions to clarify the dream scene. After a series of nonanalytical questions, the partner (or dream tracker) asks the dreamer what he wants to know, what he intends to do when he reenters the dream space, whether she can have permission to enter the dream space, and if granted, what the dreamer wants her to do once she is inside it. Moss relates that the tracker can so completely reenter the dream with the dreamer that she often comes away with knowledge of the dream that had not been shared outside the common dream.[5]

A method of group dream work psychologists often use is commonly referred to as the "If This Were My Dream" practice. It lends itself well to shared sacred or mystical dreaming. Dreamers sit in a circle and take turns sharing a dream with the group that they would like more insight on. One by one, each member of the group responds by saying, "If this were my dream ... " and then goes on to explain how he would try to analyze some of the dream imagery or metaphor. This method not only respects the instinctual prerogative of the dreamer, but opens new ideas about how to go about researching and interpreting it. For sacred dreaming, receiving insights from other members of your usual religious group or community can be valuable. I have found doing this exercise with a group of spiritual dreamers from a variety of religious backgrounds to be a particularly rich experience. However you might form your dream circle, be aware that if you plan to share sacred dreams, everyone involved must be open to the spiritual dimensions of the dream world.

Whatever you do, persevere in developing your own sacred dream spiral. Mystical dreams respond to incubation and development but still do not always come how and when we would like them to. With patience and faith, however, they do eventually come, and with mindful and heartfelt sacred dream work, they always produce astounding results and marvelous revelations. As you continue to develop your sacred art dream spiral, if you are responsive to the sacred presence that evolves through it, you will naturally fall into a spiritual flow of breathing, growing, changing, and flourishing. You will surely live your whole life with the magical and mystical quality of the sacred dream.

NOTES

INTRODUCTION

1. Kelly Bulkeley, "Mystical Dreaming: Patterns in Form, Content, and Meaning," *Dreaming* 19, no. 1 (March 2009): 30–33.

2. Fariba Bogzaran, "The Spiritual Dimensions of Lucid Dreaming," *Elixir* 3 (Autumn 2006), 29.

CHAPTER ONE

1. A. Leo Oppenheim, "The Interpretation of Dreams in the Ancient Near East, With a Translation of an Assyrian Dream-Book," *Transactions of the American Philosophical Society* 46, no. 3 (1956): 179–373.

2. Kelly Bulkeley, *Dreaming in the World's Religions: A Comparative History* (New York: New York University Press, 2008), 118.

3. Robert L. Van de Castle, *Our Dreaming Mind* (New York: Ballantine Books, 1994), 55.

4. E. A. Wallis Budge, *Egyptian Magic,* vol. 2 of *Books on Egypt and Chaldea* (London: Kegan Paul, Trench, and Trübner, 1899). Cited in Van de Castle, *Our Dreaming Mind,* 55.

5. *Chandogya Upanishad*, 5.2.4–9, trans. Patrick Olivelle (1996), 39–40.

6. Van de Castle, *Our Dreaming Mind,* 73.

7. Bulkeley, *Dreaming in the World's Religions,* 73.

8. *Acts of the Christian Martyrs,* ed. Herbert R. Musurillo (Oxford: Oxford University Press, 1972), 111.

9. Hidayet Aydar, "Istikhara and Dreams," in *Dreaming in Christianity and Islam: Culture, Conflict, and Creativity,* eds. Kelly Bulkeley, Kate Adams, and Patricia M. Davis (New Brunswick, NJ: Rutgers University Press, 2009), 128.

10. Bulkeley, *Dreaming in the World's Religions,* 139.

11. Ibid.

CHAPTER TWO

1. Lin Yatung, *The Wisdom of Laotse* (New York: Random House, 1948).

2. Barbara Tedlock, *The Shaman in the Woman's Body: Reclaiming the Feminine in Religion and Medicine* (New York: Bantam Books, 2005), 103.

3. Ibid., 104–5.

4. Terry D. Bilhartz, *Sacred Words: A Source Book on the Great Religions of the World* (New York: McGraw Hill, 2006), 404.

5. Tenzin Wangyal Rinpoche, *The Tibetan Yogas of Dream and Sleep* (Ithaca, NY: Snow Lion Publications), 20.

6. Serinity Young, *Dreaming in the Lotus: Buddhist Dream Narrative, Imagery, and Practice* (Boston: Wisdom Publications, 1999).

7. J. Allan Hobson, *Dreaming as Delirium: How the Brain Goes Out of Its Mind* (Cambridge, MA: MIT Press, 1999), 51–52.

8. Ibid., 52.

9. Susan Blackmore, *Consciousness: An Introduction*, 2nd ed. (London: Hodder Education, 2010), 382.

10. *The Upanishads*, trans. Eknath Easwaran (Tomales, CA: Nilgiri Press, 1996), 60–61.

11. Tracey L. Kahan, "Consciousness in Dreaming: A Metacognitive Approach," in *Dreams: A Reader on Religious, Cultural, and Psychological Dimensions of Dreaming*, ed. Kelly Bulkeley (New York: Palgrave, 2001), 344.

12. Ibid., 344–45. Kahan references a study performed by S. Purcell, A. Moffitt, and R. Hoffman in 1993.

13. Richard J. Smith, *Fortune-tellers and Philosophers: Divination in Traditional Chinese Society* (Boulder, CO: Westview Press, 1991), 250.

14. Connie Cockrell Kaplan, *The Woman's Book of Dreams: Dreaming as a Spiritual Practice* (Hillsboro, OR: Beyond Words Publishing, 1999), 8.

15. Allan Combs, *The Radiance of Being: Understanding the Grand Integral Vision; Living the Integral Life* (Saint Paul, MN: Paragon House, 2002), 7, 8.

16. Carl G. Jung, *The Undiscovered Self with Symbols and the Interpretation of Dreams*, trans. R. F. C. Hull (Princeton, NJ: Princeton University Press, 1990), 103.

17. Tedlock, *Shaman in the Woman's Body*, 104.

18. Ibid., 128.

19. Ibid., 127.

20. Barbara Tedlock, *Dreaming: Anthropological and Psychological Interpretations* (Santa Fe, NM: School of American Research Press, 1992).

CHAPTER THREE

1. Bulkeley, "Mystical Dreaming," 30–41.

2. Ibid., 35.

3. Ibid., 36.

4. Stephen Aizenstat, *Dream Tending* (Boulder, CO: Sounds True, 2001), CD–ROM, 1.5.

5. Bulkeley, "Mystical Dreaming," 37.

6. Ibid.

7. Fariba Bogzaran and Daniel Deslauriers, *Integral Dreaming: A Holistic Approach to Dreams* (Albany: State University of New York Press, 2012).

CHAPTER FOUR

1. Malcolm Godwin, *The Lucid Dreamer: A Waking Guide for the Traveler between Worlds* (New York: Simon and Schuster, 1994), 103.

2. Stephen LaBerge and Howard Rheingold, *Exploring the World of Lucid Dreaming* (New York: Ballantine Books, 1990), 7.

3. Ibid., 50–54.

4. Tenzin, *The Tibetan Yogas,* 73.

5. Ibid.

6. Rosemary Ellen Guiley, *Dreamwork for the Soul: A Spiritual Guide to Dream Interpretation* (New York: Berkley Books, 1998), 74.

7. Tenzin, *The Tibetan Yogas,* 38.

8. LaBerge and Rheingold, *Exploring the World of Lucid Dreaming,* 192.

9. Tenzin, *The Tibetan Yogas*, 98–100.

10. Ibid., 102.

11. Bogzaran, "The Spiritual Dimensions of Lucid Dreaming," 31.

12. LaBerge and Rheingold, *Exploring the World of Lucid Dreaming,* 94.

13. Lama Yeshe, *The Bliss of Inner Fire: Heart Practice of the Six Yogas of Naropa*, ed. Robina Courtin and Ailsa Cameron (Boston: Wisdom Publications, 1998), 83–84.

14. Guiley, *Dreamwork for the Soul*, 60.

CHAPTER FIVE

1. C. G. Jung, "On the Nature of Dreams," in *Dreams: From the Collected Works of C. G. Jung, Volumes 4, 8, 12, 16*, Bollingen Series XX, trans. R. F. C. Hull (Princeton, NJ: Princeton University Press, 1974), 76.

2. C. G. Jung, "The Structure of the Psyche," in *The Portable Jung*, ed. Joseph Campbell, trans. R. F. C. Hull (New York: Penguin Books, 1976), 26–27.

3. Michele Stephen, "Memory, Emotion, and the Imaginal Mind," in *Dreaming and the Self: New Perspectives on Subjectivity, Identity, and Emotion*, ed. Marie Mageo (Albany: State University of New York Press, 2003), 97.

4. Aizenstat, *Dream Tending*, 2.4.

5. Clifford Geertz, *The Interpretation of Cultures* (New York: Basic Books, 1973), 9–10. Geertz borrowed the term "thick description" from Gilbert Ryles.

6. Ibid., 10.

CHAPTER SIX

1. Bulkeley, *Dreaming in the World's Religions*, 54.

2. Ibid., 78.

3. Ibid., 113.

4. Scott Noegel, "Dreams and Dream Interpreters in Mesopotamia and in the Hebrew Bible," in *Dreams*, ed. Kelly Bulkeley, 50. Noegel cites an excerpt of the translation of the Epic of Gilgamesh by Stephanie Dalley, *Myths from Mesopotamia: Creation, the Flood, Gilgamesh, and Others*, Oxford World Classics (New York: Oxford University Press, 1989), 136–37.

5. Ibid.

6. Guiley, *Dreamwork for the Soul*, 121.

7. Noegel, "Dreams and Dream Interpreters," 56.

8. Marcia Hermansen, "Dreams and Dreaming in Islam," in *Dreams,* ed. Kelly Bulkeley, 76, from al-Darima's and other Hadith collections.

9. Ibn Khaldun, *The Muqaddimah: An Introduction to History,* ed. and trans. Franz Rosenthal, Bollingen Series (Princeton, NJ: Princeton University Press, 1967).

10. Bulkeley, *Dreaming in the World's Religions,* 205.

11. Hermansen, "Dreams and Dreaming in Islam," in *Dreams,* ed. Kelly Bulkeley, 76.

12. Ibid., 77–79.

13. Bulkeley, *Dreaming in the World's Religions,* 152.

14. Ibid., 154.

15. Artemidorus Daldianus, *Oneirocritica,* trans. Robert J. White (Park Ridge, NJ: Noyes Press, 1975), in Bulkeley, *Dreaming in the World's Religions,* 163.

16. Bulkeley, *Dreaming in the World's Religions,* 213.

17. Sigmund Freud, *The Letters of Sigmund Freud,* ed. Ernst L. Freud, trans. T. Stern and J. Stern (New York: Basic Books, 1960).

18. Sigmund Freud, *The Interpretation of Dreams* (New York: Basic Books, 1953).

19. C. G. Jung, *Psychology and Alchemy,* vol. 12 of *The Collected Works of C. G. Jung,* ed. and trans. Gerhard Adler and R. F. C. Hull, Bollingen Series XX (Princeton, NJ: Princeton University Press, 1993), 47–223.

20. Ibid., 289.

21. Guiley, *Dreamwork for the Soul,* 121.

22. Adele Nozedar, *The Illustrated Signs and Symbols Sourcebook: An A to Z Compendium of Over 1000 Designs* (New York: Metro Books, 2008), 72.

CHAPTER SEVEN

1. Clarissa Pinkola Estés, *Women Who Run with the Wolves: Myths and Stories of the Wild Woman Archetype* (New York: Ballantine Books, 1995), 322.

2. Van de Castle, *Our Dreaming Minds,* 11–21.

3. Nancy Grace, "Making Dreams into Music: Contemporary Songwriters Carry On an Age-Old Dreaming Tradition," in *Dreams,* ed. Kelly Bulkeley, 167–68.

4. Tedlock, *The Woman in the Shaman's Body,* 82–83.

CHAPTER EIGHT

1. Jeremy Taylor, "Group Work with Dreams: The 'Royal Road' to Meaning," in *Dreams*, ed. Kelly Bulkeley, 196.

2. Patricia Garfield, *The Healing Power of Dreams* (New York: Simon and Schuster, 1991), 34.

3. Ibid., 18.

4. Ibid., 30.

5. Ibid., 31.

6. Ibid.

7. Ibid., 37.

8. Douglas Hollan, "Selfscape Dreams" in *Dreaming and the Self*, ed. Marie Mageo, 63. Hollan cites Oliver Sacks, "Neurological Dreams," in Deirdre Barrett, ed., *Trauma and Dreams* (Cambridge, MA: Harvard University Press, 1996).

9. Ibid., 62–63.

10. LaBerge and Rheingold, *Exploring the World of Lucid Dreaming*, 207.

11. Rubin R. Naiman, *Healing Night: The Science and Spirit of Sleeping, Dreaming, and Awakening* (Minneapolis: Syren Book Company, 2006), xiv.

12. Edward Tick, *The Practice of Dream Healing: Bringing the Ancient Greek Mysteries into Modern Medicine* (Wheaton, IL: Quest Books, 2001), 158.

13. Robert Moss, *Dreaming the Soul Back Home: Shamanic Dreaming for Healing and Becoming Whole* (Novato, CA: New World Library, 2012), 61.

14. Ibid., 62–63.

15. Ibid., 80–83.

16. Ibid., 84.

17. Ibid., 89.

18. Caroline Myss, *The Anatomy of the Spirit: The Seven Stages of Power and Healing* (New York: Three Rivers Press, 1996), 103–5.

19. Ibid., 129–32.

20. Ibid., 167–69.

21. Ibid., 197–99.

22. Ibid., 219–21.

23. Ibid., 237–39.

24. Ajit Mookerjee, *Kundalini: The Arousal of the Inner Energy* (Rochester, VT: Destiny Books, 1986), 44.

25. Myss, *Anatomy of the Spirit,* 265–67.

CHAPTER NINE

1. Erika Bourguignon, "Dreams that Speak: Experience and Interpretation," in *Dreaming and the Self*, ed. Marie Mageo, 133.

2. John Boghosian Arden, *Consciousness, Dreams, and Self: A Transdisciplinary Approach* (Madison, CT: Psychosocial Press, 1996), 100.

3. Ibid., 100–101.

4. Ibid., 101.

5. Bulkeley, "Mystical Dreaming," 33 (see "Introduction," n. 1).

6. Bulkeley, *Dreaming in the World's Religions,* 21.

7. Ibid., 24.

8. Serinity Young, "Buddhist Dream Experience: The Role of Interpretation, Ritual, and Gender," in *Dreams,* ed. Kelly Bulkeley, 14, 18.

9. Ibid., 11, 13.

10. Bulkeley, *Dreaming in the World's Religions,* 128.

11. Ibid., 154.

12. Ibid.

13. Ibid., 173.

14. Lori Joan Swick, "Recognizing Women's Initiative in the Development of Christianity," (PhD diss., California Institute of Integral Studies, 2013), 137–66, ProQuest ciis 10274.

15. Bulkeley, *Dreaming in the World's Religions*, 198.

16. Ibid., 198.

17. Ibid., 198–99. Bulkeley cites the Qur'an, trans. N. J. Dawood (London: Penguin Classics, 1974).

18. Parisa Rahimian, "Women and Dream Interpretation in Contemporary Iran," in *Dreaming in Christianity and Islam*, ed. Bulkeley et al., 156.

19. Ibid., 158.

20. Ibid., 157–58.

21. Lee Irwin, "Sending a Voice, Seeking a Place: Visionary Traditions among Native Women of the Plains," in *Dreams*, ed. Kelly Bulkeley, 95.

22. Ibid., 104.

23. Young, "Dreams," *The Encyclopedia of Women and World Religions,* vol. 1 (New York: Macmillan, 1998), 271.

24. Gerda Lerner, *The Creation of Patriarchy* (New York: Oxford University Press, 1986), 8.

25. Young, "Buddhist Dream Experience," 15.

CONCLUSION

1. Daniel Deslauriers, "Dreamwork in the Light of Emotional and Spiritual Intelligence," *Journal of Advanced Development* 9 (2000): 105.

2. Ibid., 105–22.

3. Bulkeley, *Dreaming in the World's Religions,* 227.

4. Kaplan, *The Woman's Book of Dreams,* 77.

5. Moss, *Dreaming the Soul Back Home,* 108–10.

SUGGESTIONS FOR FURTHER READING

Acts of the Christian Martyrs. Edited by Herbert R. Musurillo. Oxford, UK: Oxford University Press, 1972.

Aizenstat, Stephen. *Dream Tending: Awakening to the Healing Power of Dreams.* Boulder, CO: Sounds True, 2001. CD-ROM.

Arden, John Boghosian. *Consciousness, Dreams, and Self: A Transdisciplinary Approach.* Madison, CT: Psychosocial Press, 1996.

Bilhartz, Terry D. *Sacred Words: A Source Book on the Great Religions of the World.* New York: McGraw Hill, 2006.

Blackmore, Susan. *Consciousness: An Introduction*, 2nd ed. London: Hodder Education, 2010.

Bogzaran, Fariba. "The Spiritual Dimensions of Lucid Dreaming." *Elixir* 3 (Autumn 2006): 23–32.

———— and Daniel Deslauriers. *Integral Dreaming: A Holistic Approach to Dreams.* Albany: State University of New York Press, 2012.

Bulkeley, Kelly. *Dreaming in the World's Religions: A Comparative History.* New York: New York University Press, 2008.

————, ed. *Dreams: A Reader on Religious, Cultural, and Psychological Dimensions of Dreaming.* New York: Palgrave, 2001.

————. "Mystical Dreaming: Patterns in Form, Content, and Meaning" *Dreaming* 19, no. 1 (March 2009): 30–41.

————, Kate Adams, and Patricia M. Davis, eds. *Dreaming in Christianity and Islam: Culture, Conflict, and Creativity.* New Brunswick, NJ: Rutgers University Press, 2009.

Combs, Allan. *The Radiance of Being: Understanding the Grand Integral Vision; Living the Integral Life.* Saint Paul, MN: Paragon House, 2002.

Deslauriers, Daniel. "Dreamwork in the Light of Emotional and Spiritual Intelligence." *Journal of Advanced Development* 9 (2000): 105–22.

Estés, Clarissa Pinkola. *Women Who Run with the Wolves: Myths and Stories of the Wild Woman Archetype.* New York: Ballantine Books, 1995.

Fontana, David. *The Secret Language of Symbols: A Visual Key to Symbols and Their Meanings.* San Francisco: Chronicle Books, 1994.

Freud, Sigmund. *The Interpretation of Dreams.* New York: Basic Books, 1953.

———. *The Letters of Sigmund Freud.* Edited by Ernst L. Freud. Translated by T. Stern and J. Stern. New York: Basic Books, 1960.

Garfield, Patricia. *The Healing Power of Dreams.* New York: Simon and Schuster, 1991.

Geertz, Clifford. *The Interpretation of Cultures.* New York: Basic Books, 1973.

Godwin, Malcolm. *The Lucid Dreamer: A Waking Guide for the Traveler between Worlds.* New York: Simon and Schuster, 1994.

Guiley, Rosemary Ellen. *Dreamwork for the Soul: A Spiritual Guide to Dream Interpretation.* New York: Berkley Books, 1998.

Hobson, J. Allan. *Dreaming as Delirium: How the Brain Goes Out of Its Mind.* Cambridge, MA: MIT Press, 1999.

Jung, Carl G. "On the Nature of Dreams." In *Dreams: From the Collected Works of C. G. Jung,* volumes 4, 8, 12, 16, Bollingen Series XX. Translated by R. F. C. Hull. Princeton, NJ: Princeton University Press, 1974.

———. *Psychology and Alchemy.* vol. 12 of *The Collected Works of C. G. Jung.* Edited and translated by Gerhard Adler and R. F. C. Hull. Bollingen Series XX. Princeton, NJ: Princeton University Press, 1993.

———. *The Undiscovered Self with Symbols and the Interpretation of Dreams.* Translated by R. F. C. Hull. Princeton, NJ: Princeton University Press, 1990.

Kaplan, Connie Cockrell. *The Woman's Book of Dreams: Dreaming as a Spiritual Practice.* Hillsboro, OR: Beyond Words Publishing, 1999.

LaBerge, Stephen, and Howard Rheingold. *Exploring the World of Lucid Dreaming.* New York: Ballantine Books, 1990.

Lerner, Gerda. *The Creation of Patriarchy.* New York: Oxford University Press, 1986.

Mageo, Marie, ed. *Dreaming and the Self: New Perspectives on Subjectivity, Identity, and Emotion.* Albany: State University of New York Press, 2003.

Mookerjee, Ajit. *Kundalini: The Arousal of the Inner Energy.* Rochester, VT: Destiny Books, 1986.

Moss, Robert. *Dreaming the Soul Back Home: Shamanic Dreaming for Healing and Becoming Whole.* Novato, CA: New World Library, 2012.

Myss, Caroline. *The Anatomy of the Spirit: The Seven Stages of Power and Healing.* New York: Three Rivers Press, 1996.

Naiman, Rubin R. *Healing Night: The Science and Spirit of Sleeping, Dreaming, and Awakening.* Minneapolis: Syren Book Company, 2006.

Nozedar, Adele. *The Illustrated Signs and Symbols Sourcebook: An A to Z Compendium of Over 1000 Designs.* New York: Metro Books, 2008.

Oppenheim, A. Leo. "The Interpretation of Dreams in the Ancient Near East, With a Translation of an Assyrian Dream-Book." *Transactions of the American Philosophical Society* 46, no. 3 (1956): 179–373.

Smith, Richard J. *Fortune-tellers and Philosophers: Divination in Traditional Chinese Society.* Boulder, CO: Westview Press, 1991.

Swick, Lori Joan. "Recognizing Women's Initiative in the Development of Christianity." PhD diss., California Institute of Integral Studies, 2013. ProQuest (ciis 10274).

Tedlock, Barbara. *Dreaming: Anthropological and Psychological Interpretations.* Santa Fe, NM: School of American Research Press, 1992.

———. *The Shaman in the Woman's Body: Reclaiming the Feminine in Religion and Medicine.* New York: Bantam Books, 2005.

Tenzin, Wangyal Rinpoche. *The Tibetan Yogas of Dream and Sleep.* Ithaca, NY: Snow Lion Publications, 1998.

Tick, Edward. *The Practice of Dream Healing: Bringing the Ancient Greek Mysteries into Modern Medicine.* Wheaton, IL: Quest Books, 2001.

Upanishads, The. Translated by Eknath Easwaran. Tomales, CA: Nilgiri Press, 1996.

Van de Castle, Robert L. *Our Dreaming Mind.* New York: Ballantine Books, 1994.

Walker, Barbara G. *The Woman's Dictionary of Symbols and Sacred Objects.* Edison, NJ: Castle Books, 1988.

Yatung, L. *The Wisdom of Laotse.* New York: Random House, 1948.

Yeshe, Lama. *The Bliss of Inner Fire: Heart Practice of the Six Yogas of Naropa.* Edited by Robina Courtin and Ailsa Cameron. Boston: Wisdom Publications, 1998.

Young, Serinity. *Dreaming in the Lotus: Buddhist Dream Narrative, Imagery, and Practice.* Boston: Wisdom Publications, 1999.

———. "Dreams." In *The Encyclopedia of Women and World Religions,* vol. 1. New York: Macmillan, 1998.

Inspiration

Finding God Beyond Religion: A Guide for Skeptics, Agnostics & Unorthodox Believers Inside & Outside the Church
By Tom Stella; Foreword by The Rev. Canon Marianne Wells Borg
Reinterprets traditional religious teachings central to the Christian faith for people who have outgrown the beliefs and devotional practices that once made sense to them.
6 x 9, 160 pp, Quality PB, 978-1-59473-485-4 **$16.99**

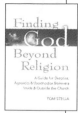

Fully Awake and Truly Alive: Spiritual Practices to Nurture Your Soul
By Rev. Jane E. Vennard; Foreword by Rami Shapiro
Illustrates the joys and frustrations of spiritual practice, offers insights from various religious traditions and provides exercises and meditations to help us become more fully alive.
6 x 9, 208 pp, Quality PB, 978-1-59473-473-1 **$16.99**

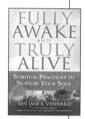

How Did I Get to Be 70 When I'm 35 Inside?: Spiritual Surprises of Later Life *By Linda Douty*
Encourages you to focus on the inner changes of aging to help you greet your later years as the grand adventure they can be. 6 x 9, 208 pp, Quality PB, 978-1-59473-297-3 **$16.99**

Journeys of Simplicity: Traveling Light with Thomas Merton, Bashō, Edward Abbey, Annie Dillard & Others *By Philip Harnden*
Invites you to consider a more graceful way of traveling through life. PB includes journal pages to help you get started on your own spiritual journey.
5 x 7¼, 144 pp, Quality PB, 978-1-59473-181-5 **$12.99**
5 x 7¼, 128 pp, HC, 978-1-893361-76-8 **$16.95**

Perennial Wisdom for the Spiritually Independent
Sacred Teachings—Annotated & Explained
Annotation by Rami Shapiro; Foreword by Richard Rohr
Weaves sacred texts and teachings from the world's major religions into a coherent exploration of the five core questions at the heart of every religion's search.
5½ x 8½, 336 pp, Quality PB Original, 978-1-59473-515-8 **$16.99**

Saving Civility: 52 Ways to Tame Rude, Crude & Attitude for a Polite Planet
By Sara Hacala
Provides fifty-two practical ways you can reverse the course of incivility and make the world a more enriching, pleasant place to live.
6 x 9, 240 pp, Quality PB, 978-1-59473-314-7 **$16.99**

Spiritually Healthy Divorce: Navigating Disruption with Insight & Hope
By Carolyne Call
A spiritual map to help you move through the twists and turns of divorce.
6 x 9, 224 pp, Quality PB, 978-1-59473-288-1 **$16.99**

Who Is My God? 2nd Edition
An Innovative Guide to Finding Your Spiritual Identity
By the Editors at SkyLight Paths
Provides the Spiritual Identity Self-Test™ to uncover the components of your unique spirituality. 6 x 9, 160 pp, Quality PB, 978-1-59473-014-6 **$15.99**

Or phone, fax, mail or e-mail to: SKYLIGHT PATHS Publishing
Sunset Farm Offices, Route 4 • P.O. Box 237 • Woodstock, Vermont 05091
Tel: (802) 457-4000 • Fax: (802) 457-4004 • www.skylightpaths.com
Credit card orders: (800) 962-4544 (8:30AM–5:30PM EST Monday–Friday)
Generous discounts on quantity orders. SATISFACTION GUARANTEED. Prices subject to change.

Bible Stories / Folktales

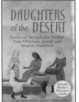

Abraham's Bind & Other Bible Tales of Trickery, Folly, Mercy and Love *By Michael J. Caduto*
New retellings of episodes in the lives of familiar biblical characters explore relevant life lessons. 6 x 9, 224 pp, HC, 978-1-59473-186-0 **$19.99**

Daughters of the Desert: Stories of Remarkable Women from Christian, Jewish and Muslim Traditions *By Claire Rudolf Murphy, Meghan Nuttall Sayres, Mary Cronk Farrell, Sarah Conover and Betsy Wharton*
Breathes new life into the old tales of our female ancestors in faith. Uses traditional scriptural passages as starting points, then with vivid detail fills in historical context and place. Chapters reveal the voices of Sarah, Hagar, Huldah, Esther, Salome, Mary Magdalene, Lydia, Khadija, Fatima and many more. Historical fiction ideal for readers of all ages.
5½ x 8½, 192 pp, Quality PB, 978-1-59473-106-8 **$14.99** Inc. reader's discussion guide

The Triumph of Eve & Other Subversive Bible Tales
By Matt Biers-Ariel
These engaging retellings of familiar Bible stories are witty, often hilarious and always profound. They invite you to grapple with questions and issues that are often hidden in the original texts.
5½ x 8½, 192 pp, Quality PB, 978-1-59473-176-1 **$14.99**

Also available: **The Triumph of Eve Teacher's Guide**
8½ x 11, 44 pp, PB, 978-1-59473-152-5 **$8.99**

Wisdom in the Telling
Finding Inspiration and Grace in Traditional Folktales and Myths Retold
By Lorraine Hartin-Gelardi
6 x 9, 192 pp, HC, 978-1-59473-185-3 **$19.99**

Religious Etiquette / Reference

How to Be a Perfect Stranger, 5th Edition: The Essential Religious Etiquette Handbook *Edited by Stuart M. Matlins and Arthur J. Magida*
The indispensable guidebook to help the well-meaning guest when visiting other people's religious ceremonies. A straightforward guide to the rituals and celebrations of the major religions and denominations in the United States and Canada from the perspective of an interested guest of any other faith, based on information obtained from authorities of each religion. Belongs in every living room, library and office. Covers:
African American Methodist Churches • Assemblies of God • Bahá'í Faith • Baptist • Buddhist • Christian Church (Disciples of Christ) • Christian Science (Church of Christ, Scientist) • Churches of Christ • Episcopalian and Anglican • Hindu • Islam • Jehovah's Witnesses • Jewish • Lutheran • Mennonite/Amish • Methodist • Mormon (Church of Jesus Christ of Latter-day Saints) • Native American/First Nations • Orthodox Churches • Pentecostal Church of God • Presbyterian • Quaker (Religious Society of Friends) • Reformed Church in America/Canada • Roman Catholic • Seventh-day Adventist • Sikh • Unitarian Universalist • United Church of Canada • United Church of Christ

"The things Miss Manners forgot to tell us about religion."
—*Los Angeles Times*

"Finally, for those inclined to undertake their own spiritual journeys ... tells visitors what to expect." —*New York Times*

6 x 9, 432 pp, Quality PB, 978-1-59473-294-2 **$19.99**

The Perfect Stranger's Guide to Funerals and Grieving Practices: A Guide to Etiquette in Other People's Religious Ceremonies *Edited by Stuart M. Matlins*
6 x 9, 240 pp, Quality PB, 978-1-893361-20-1 **$16.95**

The Perfect Stranger's Guide to Wedding Ceremonies: A Guide to Etiquette in Other People's Religious Ceremonies *Edited by Stuart M. Matlins*
6 x 9, 208 pp, Quality PB, 978-1-893361-19-5 **$16.95**

Sacred Texts—SkyLight Illuminations Series

Offers today's spiritual seeker an enjoyable entry into the great classic texts of the world's spiritual traditions. Each classic is presented in an accessible translation, with facing pages of guided commentary from experts, giving you the keys you need to understand the history, context and meaning of the text.

CHRISTIANITY

The Book of Common Prayer: A Spiritual Treasure Chest— Selections Annotated & Explained
Annotation by The Rev. Canon C. K. Robertson, PhD; Foreword by The Most Rev. Katharine Jefferts Schori; Preface by Archbishop Desmond Tutu
Makes available the riches of this spiritual treasure chest for all who are interested in deepening their life of prayer, building stronger relationships and making a difference in their world. 5½ x 8½, 208 pp, Quality PB Original, 978-1-59473-524-0 **$16.99**

Celtic Christian Spirituality: Essential Writings—Annotated & Explained
Annotation by Mary C. Earle; Foreword by John Philip Newell
Explores how the writings of this lively tradition embody the gospel.
5½ x 8½, 176 pp, Quality PB, 978-1-59473-302-4 **$16.99**

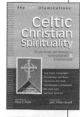

Desert Fathers and Mothers: Early Christian Wisdom Sayings— Annotated & Explained *Annotation by Christine Valters Paintner, PhD*
Opens up wisdom of the desert fathers and mothers for readers with no previous knowledge of Western monasticism and early Christianity.
5½ x 8½, 192 pp, Quality PB, 978-1-59473-373-4 **$16.99**

The End of Days: Essential Selections from Apocalyptic Texts— Annotated & Explained *Annotation by Robert G. Clouse, PhD*
Helps you understand the complex Christian visions of the end of the world.
5½ x 8½, 224 pp, Quality PB, 978-1-59473-170-9 **$16.99**

The Hidden Gospel of Matthew: Annotated & Explained
Translation & Annotation by Ron Miller
Discover the words and events that have the strongest connection to the historical Jesus.
5½ x 8½, 272 pp, Quality PB, 978-1-59473-038-2 **$16.99**

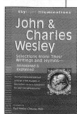

The Imitation of Christ: Selections Annotated & Explained
Annotation by Paul Wesley Chilcote, PhD; By Thomas à Kempis; Adapted from John Wesley's The Christian's Pattern
Let Jesus's example of holiness, humility and purity of heart be a companion on your own spiritual journey.
5½ x 8½, 224 pp, Quality PB, 978-1-59473-434-2 **$16.99**

The Infancy Gospels of Jesus: Apocryphal Tales from the Childhoods of Mary and Jesus—Annotated & Explained
Translation & Annotation by Stevan Davies; Foreword by A. Edward Siecienski, PhD
A startling presentation of the early lives of Mary, Jesus and other biblical figures that will amuse and surprise you. 5½ x 8½, 176 pp, Quality PB, 978-1-59473-258-4 **$16.99**

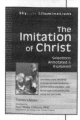

John & Charles Wesley: Selections from Their Writings and Hymns— Annotated & Explained *Annotation by Paul W. Chilcote, PhD*
A unique presentation of the writings of these two inspiring brothers brings together some of the most essential material from their large corpus of work.
5½ x 8½, 288 pp, Quality PB, 978-1-59473-309-3 **$16.99**

Julian of Norwich: Selections from *Revelations of Divine Love*—Annotated & Explained *Annotation by Mary C. Earle*
Addresses topics including the infinite nature of God, the life of prayer, God's suffering with us, the eternal and undying life of the soul, the motherhood of Jesus and the motherhood of God and more.
5½ x 8½, 160 pp (est), Quality PB Original, 978-1-59473-513-4 **$16.99**

Sacred Texts—continued

CHRISTIANITY—continued

The Lost Sayings of Jesus: Teachings from Ancient Christian, Jewish, Gnostic and Islamic Sources—Annotated & Explained
Translation & Annotation by Andrew Phillip Smith; Foreword by Stephan A. Hoeller
Depicts Jesus as a Wisdom teacher who speaks to people of all faiths as a mystic and spiritual master. 5½ x 8½, 240 pp, Quality PB, 978-1-59473-172-3 **$16.99**

Philokalia: The Eastern Christian Spiritual Texts—Selections Annotated & Explained *Annotation by Allyne Smith; Translation by G. E. H. Palmer, Phillip Sherrard and Bishop Kallistos Ware* The first approachable introduction to the wisdom of the Philokalia. 5½ x 8½, 240 pp, Quality PB, 978-1-59473-103-7 **$16.99**

The Sacred Writings of Paul: Selections Annotated & Explained
Translation & Annotation by Ron Miller Leads you into the exciting immediacy of Paul's teachings. 5½ x 8½, 224 pp, Quality PB, 978-1-59473-213-3 **$16.99**

Saint Augustine of Hippo: Selections from *Confessions* and Other Essential Writings—Annotated & Explained
Annotation by Joseph T. Kelley, PhD; Translation by the Augustinian Heritage Institute
Provides insight into the mind and heart of this foundational Christian figure.
5½ x 8½, 272 pp, Quality PB, 978-1-59473-282-9 **$16.99**

Saint Ignatius Loyola—The Spiritual Writings: Selections Annotated & Explained *Annotation by Mark Mossa, SJ* Focuses on the practical mysticism of Ignatius of Loyola. 5½ x 8½, 288 pp, Quality PB, 978-1-59473-301-7 **$16.99**

Sex Texts from the Bible: Selections Annotated & Explained
Translation & Annotation by Teresa J. Hornsby; Foreword by Amy-Jill Levine
Demystifies the Bible's ideas on gender roles, marriage, sexual orientation, virginity, lust and sexual pleasure. 5½ x 8½, 208 pp, Quality PB, 978-1-59473-217-1 **$16.99**

Spiritual Writings on Mary: Annotated & Explained
Annotation by Mary Ford-Grabowsky; Foreword by Andrew Harvey
Examines the role of Mary, the mother of Jesus, as a source of inspiration in history and in life today. 5½ x 8½, 288 pp, Quality PB, 978-1-59473-001-6 **$16.99**

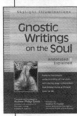

The Way of a Pilgrim: The Jesus Prayer Journey—Annotated & Explained
Translation & Annotation by Gleb Pokrovsky; Foreword by Andrew Harvey A classic of Russian Orthodox spirituality. 5½ x 8½, 160 pp, Illus., Quality PB, 978-1-893361-31-7 **$14.95**

GNOSTICISM

Gnostic Writings on the Soul: Annotated & Explained
Translation & Annotation by Andrew Phillip Smith; Foreword by Stephan A. Hoeller
Reveals the inspiring ways your soul can remember and return to its unique, divine purpose. 5½ x 8½, 144 pp, Quality PB, 978-1-59473-220-1 **$16.99**

The Gospel of Philip: Annotated & Explained
Translation & Annotation by Andrew Phillip Smith; Foreword by Stevan Davies
Reveals otherwise unrecorded sayings of Jesus and fragments of Gnostic mythology.
5½ x 8½, 160 pp, Quality PB, 978-1-59473-111-2 **$16.99**

The Gospel of Thomas: Annotated & Explained
Translation & Annotation by Stevan Davies; Foreword by Andrew Harvey
Sheds new light on the origins of Christianity and portrays Jesus as a wisdom-loving sage.
5½ x 8½, 192 pp, Quality PB, 978-1-893361-45-4 **$16.99**

The Secret Book of John: The Gnostic Gospel—Annotated & Explained
Translation & Annotation by Stevan Davies The most significant and influential text of the ancient Gnostic religion. 5½ x 8½, 208 pp, Quality PB, 978-1-59473-082-5 **$16.99**

See Inspiration for *Perennial Wisdom for the Spiritually Independent: Sacred Teachings—Annotated & Explained*

Sacred Texts—continued

JUDAISM

The Book of Job: Annotated & Explained
Translation and Annotation by Donald Kraus; Foreword by Dr. Marc Brettler
Clarifies for today's readers what Job is, how to overcome difficulties in the text, and what it may mean for us.
5½ x 8½, 256 pp, Quality PB, 978-1-59473-389-5 **$16.99**

The Divine Feminine in Biblical Wisdom Literature
Selections Annotated & Explained
Translation & Annotation by Rabbi Rami Shapiro; Foreword by Rev. Cynthia Bourgeault, PhD
Uses the Hebrew Bible and Wisdom literature to explain Sophia's way of wisdom and illustrate Her creative energy.
5½ x 8½, 240 pp, Quality PB, 978-1-59473-109-9 **$16.99**

Ecclesiastes: Annotated & Explained
Translation & Annotation by Rabbi Rami Shapiro; Foreword by Rev. Barbara Cawthorne Crafton
A timeless teaching on living well amid uncertainty and insecurity.
5½ x 8½, 160 pp, Quality PB, 978-1-59473-287-4 **$16.99**

Ethics of the Sages: *Pirke Avot*—Annotated & Explained
Translation & Annotation by Rabbi Rami Shapiro
Clarifies the ethical teachings of the early Rabbis.
5½ x 8½, 192 pp, Quality PB, 978-1-59473-207-2 **$16.99**

Hasidic Tales: Annotated & Explained
Translation & Annotation by Rabbi Rami Shapiro; Foreword by Andrew Harvey
Introduces the legendary tales of the impassioned Hasidic rabbis, presenting them as stories rather than as parables.
5½ x 8½, 240 pp, Quality PB, 978-1-893361-86-7 **$16.95**

The Hebrew Prophets: Selections Annotated & Explained
Translation & Annotation by Rabbi Rami Shapiro;
Foreword by Rabbi Zalman M. Schachter-Shalomi
5½ x 8½, 224 pp, Quality PB, 978-1-59473-037-5 **$16.99**

Maimonides—Essential Teachings on Jewish Faith & Ethics
The Book of Knowledge & the Thirteen Principles of Faith—Annotated & Explained
Translation and Annotation by Rabbi Marc D. Angel, PhD
Opens up for us Maimonides's views on the nature of God, providence, prophecy, free will, human nature, repentance and more.
5½ x 8½, 224 pp, Quality PB, 978-1-59473-311-6 **$18.99**

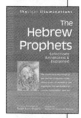

Proverbs: Annotated & Explained
Translation and Annotation by Rabbi Rami Shapiro
Demonstrates how these complex poetic forms are actually straightforward instructions to live simply, without rationalizations and excuses.
5½ x 8½, 288 pp, Quality PB, 978-1-59473-310-9 **$16.99**

Tanya, the Masterpiece of Hasidic Wisdom
Selections Annotated & Explained
Translation & Annotation by Rabbi Rami Shapiro; Foreword by Rabbi Zalman M. Schachter-Shalomi
Clarifies one of the most powerful and potentially transformative books of Jewish wisdom.
5½ x 8½, 240 pp, Quality PB, 978-1-59473-275-1 **$16.99**

Zohar: Annotated & Explained
Translation & Annotation by Daniel C. Matt; Foreword by Andrew Harvey
The canonical text of Jewish mystical tradition.
5½ x 8½, 176 pp, Quality PB, 978-1-893361-51-5 **$16.99**

See Inspiration for *Perennial Wisdom for the Spiritually Independent: Sacred Teachings—Annotated & Explained*

Sacred Texts—continued

ISLAM

Ghazali on the Principles of Islamic Spirituality
Selections from *The Forty Foundations of Religion*—Annotated & Explained
Translation & Annotation by Aaron Spevack, PhD
Makes the core message of this influential spiritual master relevant to anyone seeking a balanced understanding of Islam.
5½ x 8½, 338 pp, Quality PB, 978-1-59473-284-3 **$18.99**

The Qur'an and Sayings of Prophet Muhammad
Selections Annotated & Explained
Annotation by Sohaib N. Sultan; Translation by Yusuf Ali, Revised by Sohaib N. Sultan; Foreword by Jane I. Smith
Presents the foundational wisdom of Islam in an easy-to-use format.
5½ x 8½, 256 pp, Quality PB, 978-1-59473-222-5 **$16.99**

Rumi and Islam: Selections from His Stories, Poems, and Discourses—
Annotated & Explained *Translation & Annotation by Ibrahim Gamard*
Focuses on Rumi's place within the Sufi tradition of Islam, providing insight into the mystical side of the religion. 5½ x 8½, 240 pp, Quality PB, 978-1-59473-002-3 **$15.99**

See Inspiration for *Perennial Wisdom for the Spiritually Independent: Sacred Teachings—Annotated & Explained*

EASTERN RELIGIONS

The Art of War—Spirituality for Conflict: Annotated & Explained
By Sun Tzu; Annotation by Thomas Huynh; Translation by Thomas Huynh and the Editors at Sonshi.com; Foreword by Marc Benioff; Preface by Thomas Cleary
Highlights principles that encourage a perceptive and spiritual approach to conflict.
5½ x 8½, 256 pp, Quality PB, 978-1-59473-244-7 **$16.99**

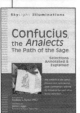

Bhagavad Gita: Annotated & Explained
Translation by Shri Purohit Swami; Annotation by Kendra Crossen Burroughs; Foreword by Andrew Harvey
Presents the classic text's teachings—with no previous knowledge of Hinduism required.
5½ x 8½, 192 pp, Quality PB, 978-1-893361-28-7 **$16.95**

Chuang-tzu: The Tao of Perfect Happiness—Selections Annotated & Explained
Translation & Annotation by Livia Kohn, PhD
Presents Taoism's central message of reverence for the "Way" of the natural world.
5½ x 8½, 240 pp, Quality PB, 978-1-59473-296-6 **$16.99**

Confucius, the *Analects:* The Path of the Sage—Selections Annotated
& Explained *Annotation by Rodney L. Taylor, PhD; Translation by James Legge, Revised by Rodney L. Taylor, PhD* Explores the ethical and spiritual meaning behind the Confucian way of learning and self-cultivation.
5½ x 8½, 192 pp, Quality PB, 978-1-59473-306-2 **$16.99**

Dhammapada: Annotated & Explained
Translation by Max Müller, revised by Jack Maguire; Annotation by Jack Maguire; Foreword by Andrew Harvey Contains all of Buddhism's key teachings, plus commentary that explains all the names, terms and references.
5½ x 8½, 160 pp, b/w photos, Quality PB, 978-1-893361-42-3 **$14.95**

Selections from the Gospel of Sri Ramakrishna: Annotated & Explained
Translation by Swami Nikhilananda; Annotation by Kendra Crossen Burroughs; Foreword by Andrew Harvey Introduces the fascinating world of the Indian mystic and the universal appeal of his message. 5½ x 8½, 240 pp, b/w photos, Quality PB, 978-1-893361-46-1 **$16.95**

Tao Te Ching: Annotated & Explained
Translation & Annotation by Derek Lin; Foreword by Lama Surya Das
Introduces an Eastern classic in an accessible, poetic and completely original way.
5½ x 8½, 208 pp, Quality PB, 978-1-59473-204-1 **$16.99**

Judaism / Christianity / Islam / Interfaith

Spiritual Gems of Islam: Insights & Practices from the Qur'an, Hadith, Rumi & Muslim Teaching Stories to Enlighten the Heart & Mind
By Imam Jamal Rahman
Invites you—no matter what your practice may be—to access the treasure chest of Islamic spirituality and use its wealth in your own journey.
6 x 9, 256 pp, Quality PB, 978-1-59473-430-4 **$16.99**

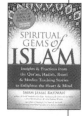

All Politics Is Religious: Speaking Faith to the Media, Policy Makers and Community *By Rabbi Dennis S. Ross; Foreword by Rev. Barry W. Lynn*
Provides ideas and strategies for expressing a clear, forceful and progressive religious point of view that is all too often overlooked and under-represented in public discourse. 6 x 9, 192 pp, Quality PB, 978-1-59473-374-1 **$18.99**

Religion Gone Astray: What We Found at the Heart of Interfaith
By Pastor Don Mackenzie, Rabbi Ted Falcon and Imam Jamal Rahman
Welcome to the deeper dimensions of interfaith dialogue—exploring that which divides us personally, spiritually and institutionally.
6 x 9, 192 pp, Quality PB, 978-1-59473-317-8 **$16.99**

Getting to the Heart of Interfaith: The Eye-Opening, Hope-Filled Friendship of a Pastor, a Rabbi & an Imam *By Pastor Don Mackenzie, Rabbi Ted Falcon and Imam Jamal Rahman*
6 x 9, 192 pp, Quality PB, 978-1-59473-263-8 **$16.99**

Hearing the Call across Traditions: Readings on Faith and Service
Edited by Adam Davis; Foreword by Eboo Patel
6 x 9, 352 pp, Quality PB, 978-1-59473-303-1 **$18.99**

How to Do Good & Avoid Evil: A Global Ethic from the Sources of Judaism
By Hans Küng and Rabbi Walter Homolka; Translated by Rev. Dr. John Bowden
6 x 9, 224 pp, HC, 978-1-59473-255-3 **$19.99**

Blessed Relief: What Christians Can Learn from Buddhists about Suffering
By Gordon Peerman 6 x 9, 208 pp, Quality PB, 978-1-59473-252-2 **$16.99**

Christians & Jews—Faith to Faith: Tragic History, Promising Present, Fragile Future *By Rabbi James Rudin*
6 x 9, 288 pp, HC, 978-1-58023-432-0 **$24.99*** Quality PB, 978-1-58023-717-8 **$18.99***

Christians & Jews in Dialogue: Learning in the Presence of the Other *By Mary C. Boys and Sara S. Lee; Foreword by Dorothy C. Bass* 6 x 9, 240 pp, Quality PB, 978-1-59473-254-6 **$18.99**

InterActive Faith: The Essential Interreligious Community-Building Handbook
Edited by Rev. Bud Heckman with Rori Picker Neiss; Foreword by Rev. Dirk Ficca
6 x 9, 304 pp, Quality PB, 978-1-59473-273-7 **$16.99**; HC, 978-1-59473-237-9 **$29.99**

The Jewish Approach to God: A Brief Introduction for Christians
By Rabbi Neil Gillman, PhD 5½ x 8½, 192 pp, Quality PB, 978-1-58023-190-9 **$16.95***

The Jewish Approach to Repairing the World (Tikkun Olam): A Brief Introduction for Christians *By Rabbi Elliot N. Dorff, PhD, with Rev. Cory Willson*
5½ x 8½, 256 pp, Quality PB, 978-1-58023-349-1 **$16.99***

The Jewish Connection to Israel, the Promised Land: A Brief Introduction for Christians *By Rabbi Eugene Korn, PhD* 5½ x 8½, 192 pp, Quality PB, 978-1-58023-318-7 **$14.99***

Jewish Holidays: A Brief Introduction for Christians *By Rabbi Kerry M. Olitzky and Rabbi Daniel Judson* 5½ x 8½, 176 pp, Quality PB, 978-1-58023-302-6 **$16.99***

Jewish Ritual: A Brief Introduction for Christians
By Rabbi Kerry M. Olitzky and Rabbi Daniel Judson 5½ x 8½, 144 pp, Quality PB, 978-1-58023-210-4 **$14.99***

Jewish Spirituality: A Brief Introduction for Christians *By Rabbi Lawrence Kushner*
5½ x 8½, 112 pp, Quality PB, 978-1-58023-150-3 **$12.95***

* A book from Jewish Lights, SkyLight Paths' sister imprint

Children's Spirituality

ENDORSED BY CATHOLIC, PROTESTANT, JEWISH, AND BUDDHIST RELIGIOUS LEADERS

Remembering My Grandparent: A Kid's Own Grief Workbook in the Christian Tradition *By Nechama Liss-Levinson, PhD, and Rev. Molly Phinney Baskette, MDiv* 8 x 10, 48 pp, 2-color text, HC, 978-1-59473-212-6 **$16.99** *For ages 7 & up*

Does God Ever Sleep? *By Joan Sauro, CSJ*
A charming nighttime reminder that God is always present in our lives.
10 x 8½, 32 pp, Full-color photos, Quality PB, 978-1-59473-110-5 **$8.99** *For ages 3–6*

Does God Forgive Me? *By August Gold; Full-color photos by Diane Hardy Waller*
Gently shows how God forgives all that we do if we are truly sorry.
10 x 8½, 32 pp, Full-color photos, Quality PB, 978-1-59473-142-6 **$8.99** *For ages 3–6*

God Said Amen *By Sandy Eisenberg Sasso; Full-color illus. by Avi Katz*
A warm and inspiring tale that shows us that we need only reach out to each other to find the answers to our prayers.
9 x 12, 32 pp, Full-color illus., HC, 978-1-58023-080-3 **$16.95*** *For ages 4 & up*

How Does God Listen? *By Kay Lindahl; Full-color photos by Cynthia Maloney*
How do we know when God is listening to us? Children will find the answers to these questions as they engage their senses while the story unfolds, learning how God listens in the wind, waves, clouds, hot chocolate, perfume, our tears and our laughter.
10 x 8½, 32 pp, Full-color photos, Quality PB, 978-1-59473-084-9 **$8.99** *For ages 3–6*

In God's Hands *By Lawrence Kushner and Gary Schmidt; Full-color illus. by Matthew J. Baek*
A delightful, timeless legend that tells of the ordinary miracles that occur when we really, truly open our eyes to the world around us.
9 x 12, 32 pp, Full-color illus., HC, 978-1-58023-224-1 **$16.99*** *For ages 5 & up*

In God's Name *By Sandy Eisenberg Sasso; Full-color illus. by Phoebe Stone*
Like an ancient myth in its poetic text and vibrant illustrations, this award-winning modern fable about the search for God's name celebrates the diversity and, at the same time, the unity of all the people of the world.
9 x 12, 32 pp, Full-color illus., HC, 978-1-879045-26-2 **$16.99*** *For ages 4 & up*

Also available in Spanish: El nombre de Dios
9 x 12, 32 pp, Full-color illus., HC, 978-1-893361-63-8 **$16.95**

In Our Image: God's First Creatures
By Nancy Sohn Swartz; Full-color illus. by Melanie Hall
A playful new twist on the Genesis story—from the perspective of the animals. Celebrates the interconnectedness of nature and the harmony of all living things.
9 x 12, 32 pp, Full-color illus., HC, 978-1-879045-99-6 **$16.95*** *For ages 4 & up*
Animated app available on Apple App Store and the Google Play marketplace **$9.99**

Noah's Wife: The Story of Naamah
By Sandy Eisenberg Sasso; Full-color illus. by Bethanne Andersen
Opens young readers' religious imaginations to new ideas about the well-known story of the Flood. When God tells Noah to bring the animals of the world onto the ark, God also calls on Naamah, Noah's wife, to save each plant on Earth.
9 x 12, 32 pp, Full-color illus., HC, 978-1-58023-134-3 **$16.95*** *For ages 4 & up*

Also available: Naamah: Noah's Wife (A Board Book)
By Sandy Eisenberg Sasso; Full-color illus. by Bethanne Andersen
5 x 5, 24 pp, Full-color illus., Board Book, 978-1-893361-56-0 **$7.95** *For ages 1–4*

Where Does God Live? *By August Gold and Matthew J. Perlman*
Helps children and their parents find God in the world around us with simple, practical examples children can relate to.
10 x 8½, 32 pp, Full-color photos, Quality PB, 978-1-893361-39-3 **$8.99** *For ages 3–6*

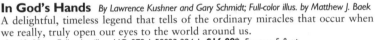

* A book from Jewish Lights, SkyLight Paths' sister imprint

Prayer / Meditation

Men Pray: Voices of Strength, Faith, Healing, Hope and Courage
Created by the Editors at SkyLight Paths
Celebrates the rich variety of ways men around the world have called out to the Divine—with words of joy, praise, gratitude, wonder, petition and even anger—from the ancient world up to our own day.
5 x 7¼, 192 pp, HC, 978-1-59473-395-6 **$16.99**

Honest to God Prayer: Spirituality as Awareness, Empowerment, Relinquishment and Paradox
By Kent Ira Groff
For those turned off by shopworn religious language, offers innovative ways to pray based on both Native American traditions and Ignatian spirituality.
6 x 9, 192 pp, Quality PB, 978-1-59473-433-5 **$16.99**

Sacred Attention: A Spiritual Practice for Finding God in the Moment
By Margaret D. McGee
Framed on the Christian liturgical year, this inspiring guide explores ways to develop a practice of attention as a means of talking—and listening—to God.
6 x 9, 144 pp, Quality PB, 978-1-59473-291-1 **$16.99**

Women of Color Pray: Voices of Strength, Faith, Healing, Hope and Courage
Edited and with Introductions by Christal M. Jackson
Through these prayers, poetry, lyrics, meditations and affirmations, you will share in the strong and undeniable connection women of color share with God.
5 x 7¼, 208 pp, Quality PB, 978-1-59473-077-1 **$15.99**

Living into Hope: A Call to Spiritual Action for Such a Time as This
By Rev. Dr. Joan Brown Campbell; Foreword by Karen Armstrong
6 x 9, 208 pp, Quality PB, 978-1-59473-436-6 **$18.99**
HC, 978-1-59473-283-6 **$21.99**

Praying with Our Hands: 21 Practices of Embodied Prayer from the World's Spiritual Traditions *By Jon M. Sweeney; Photos by Jennifer J. Wilson; Foreword by Mother Tessa Bielecki; Afterword by Taitetsu Unno, PhD*
8 x 8, 96 pp, 22 duotone photos, Quality PB, 978-1-893361-16-4 **$16.95**

Secrets of Prayer: A Multifaith Guide to Creating Personal Prayer in Your Life
By Nancy Corcoran, CSJ
6 x 9, 160 pp, Quality PB, 978-1-59473-215-7 **$16.99**

Three Gates to Meditation Practice: A Personal Journey into Sufism, Buddhism, and Judaism *By David A. Cooper* 5½ x 8½, 240 pp, Quality PB, 978-1-893361-22-5 **$18.99**

Prayer / M. Basil Pennington, OCSO

Finding Grace at the Center, 3rd Edition: The Beginning of Centering Prayer *With Thomas Keating, OCSO, and Thomas E. Clarke, SJ; Foreword by Rev. Cynthia Bourgeault, PhD* A practical guide to a simple and beautiful form of meditative prayer. 5 x 7¼, 128 pp, Quality PB, 978-1-59473-182-2 **$12.99**

The Monks of Mount Athos: A Western Monk's Extraordinary Spiritual Journey on Eastern Holy Ground *Foreword by Archimandrite Dionysios*
Explores the landscape, monastic communities and food of Athos.
6 x 9, 352 pp, Quality PB, 978-1-893361-78-2 **$18.95**

Psalms: A Spiritual Commentary *Illus. by Phillip Ratner*
Reflections on some of the most beloved passages from the Bible's most widely read book. 6 x 9, 176 pp, 24 full-page b/w illus., Quality PB, 978-1-59473-234-8 **$16.99**

The Song of Songs: A Spiritual Commentary *Illus. by Phillip Ratner*
Explore the Bible's most challenging mystical text.
6 x 9, 160 pp, 14 full-page b/w illus., Quality PB, 978-1-59473-235-5 **$16.99**
HC, 978-1-59473-004-7 **$19.99**

Spirituality / Animal Companions

Blessing the Animals
Prayers and Ceremonies to Celebrate God's Creatures, Wild and Tame
Edited and with Introductions by Lynn L. Caruso
5¼ x 7¼, 256 pp, Quality PB, 978-1-59473-253-9 **$15.99**; HC, 978-1-59473-145-7 **$19.99**

Remembering My Pet
A Kid's Own Spiritual Workbook for When a Pet Dies
By Nechama Liss-Levinson, PhD, and Rev. Molly Phinney Baskette, MDiv
Foreword by Lynn L. Caruso
8 x 10, 48 pp, 2-color text, HC, 978-1-59473-221-8 **$16.99**

What Animals Can Teach Us about Spirituality
Inspiring Lessons from Wild and Tame Creatures
By Diana L. Guerrero 6 x 9, 176 pp, Quality PB, 978-1-893361-84-3 **$16.95**

Spirituality & Crafts

Beading—The Creative Spirit
Finding Your Sacred Center through the Art of Beadwork
By Rev. Wendy Ellsworth
Invites you on a spiritual pilgrimage into the kaleidoscope world of glass and color.
7 x 9, 240 pp, 8-page color insert, 40+ b/w photos and 40 diagrams, Quality PB, 978-1-59473-267-6 **$18.99**

Contemplative Crochet
A Hands-On Guide for Interlocking Faith and Craft
By Cindy Crandall-Frazier; Foreword by Linda Skolnik
Illuminates the spiritual lessons you can learn through crocheting.
7 x 9, 208 pp, b/w photos, Quality PB, 978-1-59473-238-6 **$16.99**

The Knitting Way
A Guide to Spiritual Self-Discovery
By Linda Skolnik and Janice MacDaniels
Examines how you can explore and strengthen your spiritual life through knitting.
7 x 9, 240 pp, b/w photos, Quality PB, 978-1-59473-079-5 **$16.99**

The Painting Path
Embodying Spiritual Discovery through Yoga, Brush and Color
By Linda Novick; Foreword by Richard Segalman
Explores the divine connection you can experience through art.
7 x 9, 208 pp, 8-page color insert, plus b/w photos, Quality PB, 978-1-59473-226-3 **$18.99**

The Quilting Path
A Guide to Spiritual Discovery through Fabric, Thread and Kabbalah
By Louise Silk
Explores how to cultivate personal growth through quilt making.
7 x 9, 192 pp, b/w photos and illus., Quality PB, 978-1-59473-206-5 **$16.99**

The Scrapbooking Journey
A Hands-On Guide to Spiritual Discovery
By Cory Richardson-Lauve; Foreword by Stacy Julian
Reveals how this craft can become a practice used to deepen and shape your life.
7 x 9, 176 pp, 8-page color insert, plus b/w photos, Quality PB, 978-1-59473-216-4 **$18.99**

The Soulwork of Clay
A Hands-On Approach to Spirituality
By Marjory Zoet Bankson; Photos by Peter Bankson
Takes you through the seven-step process of making clay into a pot, drawing parallels at each stage to the process of spiritual growth.
7 x 9, 192 pp, b/w photos, Quality PB, 978-1-59473-249-2 **$16.99**

Women's Interest

Birthing God: Women's Experiences of the Divine
By Lana Dalberg; Foreword by Kathe Schaaf
Powerful narratives of suffering, love and hope that inspire both personal and collective transformation. 6 x 9, 304 pp, Quality PB, 978-1-59473-480-9 **$18.99**

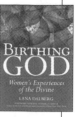

On the Chocolate Trail: A Delicious Adventure Connecting Jews, Religions, History, Travel, Rituals and Recipes to the Magic of Cacao
By Rabbi Deborah R. Prinz
Take a delectable journey through the religious history of chocolate—a real treat!
6 x 9, 272 pp, 20+ b/w photographs, Quality PB, 978-1-58023-487-0 **$18.99***

Women, Spirituality and Transformative Leadership
Where Grace Meets Power
Edited by Kathe Schaaf, Kay Lindahl, Kathleen S. Hurty, PhD, and Reverend Guo Cheen
A dynamic conversation on the power of women's spiritual leadership and its emerging patterns of transformation.
6 x 9, 288 pp, Quality PB, 978-1-59473-548-6 **$18.99**; HC, 978-1-59473-313-0 **$24.99**

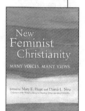

Spiritually Healthy Divorce: Navigating Disruption with Insight & Hope
By Carolyne Call A spiritual map to help you move through the twists and turns of divorce. 6 x 9, 224 pp, Quality PB, 978-1-59473-288-1 **$16.99**

New Feminist Christianity: Many Voices, Many Views
Edited by Mary E. Hunt and Diann L. Neu
Insights from ministers and theologians, activists and leaders, artists and liturgists offer a starting point for building new models of religious life and worship.
6 x 9, 384 pp, Quality PB, 978-1-59473-435-9 **$19.99**; HC, 978-1-59473-285-0 **$24.99**

Bread, Body, Spirit: Finding the Sacred in Food
Edited and with Introductions by Alice Peck 6 x 9, 224 pp, Quality PB, 978-1-59473-242-3 **$19.99**

Dance—The Sacred Art: The Joy of Movement as a Spiritual Practice
By Cynthia Winton-Henry 5½ x 8½, 224 pp, Quality PB, 978-1-59473-268-3 **$16.99**

Daughters of the Desert: Stories of Remarkable Women from Christian, Jewish and Muslim Traditions
By Claire Rudolf Murphy, Meghan Nuttall Sayres, Mary Cronk Farrell, Sarah Conover and Betsy Wharton
5½ x 8½, 192 pp, Illus., Quality PB, 978-1-59473-106-8 **$14.99** Inc. reader's discussion guide

The Divine Feminine in Biblical Wisdom Literature
Selections Annotated & Explained
Translation & Annotation by Rabbi Rami Shapiro; Foreword by Rev. Cynthia Bourgeault, PhD
5½ x 8½, 240 pp, Quality PB, 978-1-59473-109-9 **$16.99**

Divining the Body: Reclaim the Holiness of Your Physical Self
By Jan Phillips 8 x 8, 256 pp, Quality PB, 978-1-59473-080-1 **$18.99**

Honoring Motherhood: Prayers, Ceremonies & Blessings
Edited and with Introductions by Lynn L. Caruso
5 x 7¼, 272 pp, Quality PB, 978-1-58473-384-0 **$9.99**; HC, 978-1-59473-239-3 **$19.99**

Next to Godliness: Finding the Sacred in Housekeeping
Edited by Alice Peck 6 x 9, 224 pp, Quality PB, 978-1-59473-214-0 **$19.99**

ReVisions: Seeing Torah through a Feminist Lens
By Rabbi Elyse Goldstein 5½ x 8½, 224 pp, Quality PB, 978-1-58023-117-6 **$16.95***

The Triumph of Eve & Other Subversive Bible Tales
By Matt Biers-Ariel 5½ x 8½, 192 pp, Quality PB, 978-1-59473-176-1 **$14.99**

White Fire: A Portrait of Women Spiritual Leaders in America
By Malka Drucker; Photos by Gay Block 7 x 10, 320 pp, b/w photos, HC, 978-1-893361-64-5 **$24.95**

Woman Spirit Awakening in Nature: Growing Into the Fullness of Who You Are
By Nancy Barrett Chickerneo, PhD; Foreword by Eileen Fisher
8 x 8, 224 pp, b/w illus., Quality PB, 978-1-59473-250-8 **$16.99**

Women of Color Pray: Voices of Strength, Faith, Healing, Hope and Courage
Edited and with Introductions by Christal M. Jackson
5 x 7¼, 208 pp, Quality PB, 978-1-59473-077-1 **$15.99**

* A book from Jewish Lights, SkyLight Paths' sister imprint

Spirituality

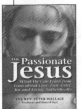

The Passionate Jesus: What We Can Learn from Jesus about Love, Fear, Grief, Joy and Living Authentically
By The Rev. Peter Wallace
Reveals Jesus as a passionate figure who was involved, present, connected, honest and direct with others and encourages you to build personal authenticity in every area of your own life. 6 x 9, 208 pp, Quality PB, 978-1-59473-393-2 **$18.99**

Gathering at God's Table: The Meaning of Mission in the Feast of Faith
By Katharine Jefferts Schori
A profound reminder of our role in the larger frame of God's dream for a restored and reconciled world. 6 x 9, 256 pp, HC, 978-1-59473-316-1 **$21.99**

The Heartbeat of God: Finding the Sacred in the Middle of Everything
By Katharine Jefferts Schori; Foreword by Joan Chittister, OSB Explores our connections to other people, to other nations and with the environment through the lens of faith. 6 x 9, 240 pp, HC, 978-1-59473-292-8 **$21.99**

A Dangerous Dozen: Twelve Christians Who Threatened the Status Quo but Taught Us to Live Like Jesus
By the Rev. Canon C. K. Robertson, PhD; Foreword by Archbishop Desmond Tutu
Profiles twelve visionary men and women who challenged society and showed the world a different way of living. 6 x 9, 208 pp, Quality PB, 978-1-59473-298-0 **$16.99**

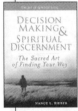

Decision Making & Spiritual Discernment: The Sacred Art of Finding Your Way *By Nancy L. Bieber*
Presents three essential aspects of Spirit-led decision making: willingness, attentiveness and responsiveness. 5½ x 8½, 208 pp, Quality PB, 978-1-59473-289-8 **$16.99**

Laugh Your Way to Grace: Reclaiming the Spiritual Power of Humor
By Rev. Susan Sparks A powerful, humorous case for laughter as a spiritual, healing path.
6 x 9, 176 pp, Quality PB, 978-1-59473-280-5 **$16.99**

Bread, Body, Spirit: Finding the Sacred in Food
Edited and with Introductions by Alice Peck 6 x 9, 224 pp, Quality PB, 978-1-59473-242-3 **$19.99**

Claiming Earth as Common Ground: The Ecological Crisis through the Lens of Faith
By Andrea Cohen-Kiener; Foreword by Rev. Sally Bingham 6 x 9, 192 pp, Quality PB, 978-1-59473-261-4 **$16.99**

Creating a Spiritual Retirement: A Guide to the Unseen Possibilities in Our Lives
By Molly Srode 6 x 9, 208 pp, b/w photos, Quality PB, 978-1-59473-050-4 **$14.99**

Creative Aging: Rethinking Retirement and Non-Retirement in a Changing World
By Marjory Zoet Bankson 6 x 9, 160 pp, Quality PB, 978-1-59473-281-2 **$16.99**

Keeping Spiritual Balance as We Grow Older: More than 65 Creative Ways to Use Purpose, Prayer, and the Power of Spirit to Build a Meaningful Retirement
By Molly and Bernie Srode 8 x 8, 224 pp, Quality PB, 978-1-59473-042-9 **$16.99**

Hearing the Call across Traditions: Readings on Faith and Service
Edited by Adam Davis; Foreword by Eboo Patel 6 x 9, 352 pp, Quality PB, 978-1-59473-303-1 **$18.99**

Honoring Motherhood: Prayers, Ceremonies & Blessings
Edited and with Introductions by Lynn L. Caruso
5 x 7¼, 272 pp, Quality PB, 978-1-58473-384-0 **$9.99**; HC, 978-1-59473-239-3 **$19.99**

The Losses of Our Lives: The Sacred Gifts of Renewal in Everyday Loss
By Dr. Nancy Copeland-Payton 6 x 9, 192 pp, HC, 978-1-59473-271-3 **$19.99**

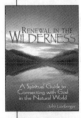

Renewal in the Wilderness: A Spiritual Guide to Connecting with God in the Natural World
By John Lionberger 6 x 9, 176 pp, b/w photos, Quality PB, 978-1-59473-219-5 **$16.99**

Soul Fire: Accessing Your Creativity
By Thomas Ryan, CSP 6 x 9, 160 pp, Quality PB, 978-1-59473-243-0 **$16.99**

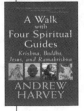

A Spirituality for Brokenness: Discovering Your Deepest Self in Difficult Times
By Terry Taylor 6 x 9, 176 pp, Quality PB, 978-1-59473-229-4 **$16.99**

A Walk with Four Spiritual Guides: Krishna, Buddha, Jesus, and Ramakrishna
By Andrew Harvey 5½ x 8½ 192 pp, b/w photos & illus., Quality PB, 978-1-59473-138-9 **$15.99**

Spiritual Practice

Fly-Fishing—The Sacred Art: Casting a Fly as a Spiritual Practice
By Rabbi Eric Eisenkramer and Rev. Michael Attas, MD; Foreword by Chris Wood, CEO, Trout Unlimited; Preface by Lori Simon, executive director, Casting for Recovery
Shares what fly-fishing can teach you about reflection, awe and wonder; the benefits of solitude; the blessing of community and the search for the Divine.
5½ x 8½, 160 pp, Quality PB, 978-1-59473-299-7 **$16.99**

Lectio Divina—The Sacred Art: Transforming Words & Images into Heart-Centered Prayer *By Christine Valters Paintner, PhD*
Expands the practice of sacred reading beyond scriptural texts and makes it accessible in contemporary life. 5½ x 8½, 240 pp, Quality PB, 978-1-59473-300-0 **$16.99**

Writing—The Sacred Art: Beyond the Page to Spiritual Practice
By Rami Shapiro and Aaron Shapiro
Push your writing through the trite and the boring to something fresh, something transformative. Includes over fifty unique, practical exercises.
5½ x 8½, 192 pp, Quality PB, 978-1-59473-372-7 **$16.99**

Conversation—The Sacred Art: Practicing Presence in an Age of Distraction
By Diane M. Millis, PhD; Foreword by Rev. Tilden Edwards, PhD
Cultivate the potential for deeper connection in every conversation.
5½ x 8½, 192 pp, Quality PB, 978-1-59473-474-8 **$16.99**

Pilgrimage—The Sacred Art: Journey to the Center of the Heart
By Dr. Sheryl A. Kujawa-Holbrook
Explore the many dimensions of the experience of pilgrimage—the yearning heart, the painful setbacks, the encounter with the Divine and, ultimately, the changed orientation to the world. 5½ x 8½, 240 pp, Quality PB, 978-1-59473-472-4 **$16.99**

Dance—The Sacred Art: The Joy of Movement as a Spiritual Practice
By Cynthia Winton-Henry 5½ x 8½, 224 pp, Quality PB, 978-1-59473-268-3 **$16.99**

Giving—The Sacred Art: Creating a Lifestyle of Generosity
By Lauren Tyler Wright 5½ x 8½, 208 pp, Quality PB, 978-1-59473-224-9 **$16.99**

Haiku—The Sacred Art: A Spiritual Practice in Three Lines
By Margaret D. McGee 5½ x 8½, 192 pp, Quality PB, 978-1-59473-269-0 **$16.99**

Hospitality—The Sacred Art: Discovering the Hidden Spiritual Power of Invitation and Welcome *By Rev. Nanette Sawyer; Foreword by Rev. Dirk Ficca*
5½ x 8½, 208 pp, Quality PB, 978-1-59473-228-7 **$16.99**

Labyrinths from the Outside In, 2nd Edition: Walking to Spiritual Insight—A Beginner's Guide *By Rev. Dr. Donna Schaper and Rev. Dr. Carole Ann Camp*
6 x 9, 208 pp, b/w illus. and photos, Quality PB, 978-1-59473-486-1 **$16.99**

Practicing the Sacred Art of Listening: A Guide to Enrich Your Relationships and Kindle Your Spiritual Life *By Kay Lindahl* 8 x 8, 176 pp, Quality PB, 978-1-893361-85-0 **$18.99**

Recovery—The Sacred Art: The Twelve Steps as Spiritual Practice *by Rami Shapiro; Foreword by Joan Borysenko, PhD* 5½ x 8½, 240 pp, Quality PB, 978-1-59473-259-1 **$16.99**

Running—The Sacred Art: Preparing to Practice *By Dr. Warren A. Kay; Foreword by Kristin Armstrong* 5½ x 8½, 160 pp, Quality PB, 978-1-59473-227-0 **$16.99**

The Sacred Art of Chant: Preparing to Practice
By Ana Hernández 5½ x 8½, 192 pp, Quality PB, 978-1-59473-036-8 **$16.99**

The Sacred Art of Fasting: Preparing to Practice
By Thomas Ryan, CSP 5½ x 8½, 192 pp, Quality PB, 978-1-59473-078-8 **$15.99**

The Sacred Art of Forgiveness: Forgiving Ourselves and Others through God's Grace
By Marcia Ford 8 x 8, 176 pp, Quality PB, 978-1-59473-175-4 **$18.99**

The Sacred Art of Listening: Forty Reflections for Cultivating a Spiritual Practice
By Kay Lindahl; Illus. by Amy Schnapper 8 x 8, 160 pp, b/w illus., Quality PB, 978-1-893361-44-7 **$16.99**

The Sacred Art of Lovingkindness: Preparing to Practice
By Rabbi Rami Shapiro; Foreword by Marcia Ford 5½ x 8½, 176 pp, Quality PB, 978-1-59473-151-8 **$16.99**

Thanking & Blessing—The Sacred Art: Spiritual Vitality through Gratefulness
By Jay Marshall, PhD; Foreword by Philip Gulley 5½ x 8½, 176 pp, Quality PB, 978-1-59473-231-7 **$16.99**

About SKYLIGHT PATHS Publishing

SkyLight Paths Publishing is creating a place where people of different spiritual traditions come together for challenge and inspiration, a place where we can help each other understand the mystery that lies at the heart of our existence.

Through spirituality, our religious beliefs are increasingly becoming a part of our lives—rather than *apart* from our lives. While many of us may be more interested than ever in spiritual growth, we may be less firmly planted in traditional religion. Yet, we do want to deepen our relationship to the sacred, to learn from our own as well as from other faith traditions, and to practice in new ways.

SkyLight Paths sees both believers and seekers as a community that increasingly transcends traditional boundaries of religion and denomination—people wanting to learn from each other, *walking together, finding the way.*

For your information and convenience, at the back of this book we have provided a list of other SkyLight Paths books you might find interesting and useful. They cover the following subjects:

Buddhism / Zen	Global Spiritual	Monasticism
Catholicism	Perspectives	Mysticism
Children's Books	Gnosticism	Poetry
Christianity	Hinduism /	Prayer
Comparative	Vedanta	Religious Etiquette
Religion	Inspiration	Retirement
Current Events	Islam / Sufism	Spiritual Biography
Earth-Based	Judaism	Spiritual Direction
Spirituality	Kabbalah	Spirituality
Enneagram	Meditation	Women's Interest
	Midrash Fiction	Worship